QUEST FOR WHOLENESS
HEALING THE BROKEN

QUEST FOR WHOLENESS

HEALING THE BROKEN

Pat Domangue

AMBASSADOR INTERNATIONAL
GREENVILLE, SOUTH CAROLINA & BELFAST, NORTHERN IRELAND

www.ambassador-international.com

QUEST FOR WHOLENESS
HEALING THE BROKEN

Printed in the United States of America

ISBN 978-1-932307-12-2

Cover Design & Page Layout by David Siglin of A&E Media

AMBASSADOR INTERNATIONAL
Emerald House
427 Wade Hampton Blvd.
Greenville, SC 29609, USA
www.ambassador-international.com

AMBASSADOR PUBLICATIONS
Providence House
Ardenlee Street
Belfast, BT6 8QJ, Northern Ireland, UK
www.ambassador-productions.com

The colophon is a trademark of Ambassador

Dedication

This Bible study is dedicated to my Lord and Savior, Jesus Christ, who made me whole, to my mother, Lou Nell Taylor, who helped me correct and complete this study, to my friend, Dr. Amy Givler, who walked me through writing the proposal, and to my mentor, Susan Hoffman, who would not let me give up.

Introduction

PSALM 42:11
Why art thou cast down, O my soul?
And why art thou disquieted within me?
Hope thou in God:
For I shall yet praise him,
Who is the health of my countenance, and my God.

"Man, my head hurts," Sandy thought as she stood for the opening song in church that morning. "I shouldn't have opened that second bottle of wine last night." The praise music to a holy God forced the guilt and shame from a lifetime of past mistakes to rise to the surface like oil poured into water. Sandy scanned the room for a sign that she was not alone, that someone else did not have it together any more than she did. She did not find what she was looking for, only reassurance she was the one person God could not change because she had been too bad for too long. Sandy noticed Georgia, a frail young woman with a scarf covering her bald head due to her cancer treatments. Georgia held the hand of her three year old son while her husband held their baby girl. Sandy wondered if this was the plight of Christians to live with diseases and broken lives. Do you know Sandy? Can you relate to the frail young woman? Is there healing for such brokenness? Do you have an area of your life that needs healing? If so, *Quest For Wholeness* is for you.

Quest For Wholeness paves the road for the Christian woman searching for healing. Whether a sick body, broken heart, a contaminated mind, or a spirit searching for peace, this study is designed to be a tool directing her to wholeness.

At some point in my life, I have been all of these. Five years I lived as a believer in Christ but did not know the brokenness in my life from past hurts and bad decisions could be transformed. At thirteen I was raped and two weeks after attempted suicide. Three years later, forced to make a decision between abortion or marriage, I walked the aisle dressed in white and soon miscarried. At nineteen, I married again, this time in pale blue. My twenties were littered with alcohol, occult books, and a never ending search for something or someone that would change my life. At thirty years old, for the third time, I said, "I do" to a wonderful man, and six months later I met "Mr. Right." His name was Jesus Christ.

For the first time I learned the true meaning of what I had been taught in Sunday School growing up. *"For God so loved the world that He gave His only begotten Son that "whosoever" believed in Him would not perish, but have everlasting life." (John 3:16)* The word "whosoever" is in quotation marks because that's where I got hung up. Could whosoever include someone like me? For the longest, I thought that whosoever meant only the "good people". God's word in *Isaiah 64:6* says *"we are all like an unclean thing, and all our righteousness are like filthy rags."* Even "good people" don't have more to offer than I do. Praise God! There is hope for us, "not so good people."

This seven week, healing journey investigates wholeness that is ours to possess as a result of a personal relationship with Jesus Christ. This study began about six years ago and grew out of my personal search into the name of God, Jehovah Rapha, meaning the Lord God who heals. I discovered His work of healing in my spiritual and emotional life and soon put my faith to the test in my physical life believing Him for relief from a painful neck problem. Once again, He healed me. I am believing God to do a healing work that transforms your life as He has mine.

Week One: Faith

Faith – "belief in, devotion to, or trust in somebody or something, especially without logical proof"

Faith is foundational for all we will learn and discuss in this study. It is the essence of who we are, who we will become, and a required ingredient for true healing. I will be using the New King James Version unless otherwise specified.

DAY 1: BY FAITH

2 THESSALONIANS 1:11-12

Therefore we also pray always for you that our God would count you worthy of this calling, and fulfill all the good pleasure of His goodness and the work of faith with power, that the name of our Lord Jesus Christ may be glorified in you, and you in Him, according to the grace of our God and the Lord Jesus Christ.

Please stop and pray this prayer.

Dear Heavenly Father,

I am about to read Your Word, and I desire to fully understand what You want me to hear. Please clear my mind, and prepare me to receive Your words. Thank You that Your Word changes me and my life for the better. In Jesus name I pray. Amen.

Today we will spend our time in Hebrews 11 which is near the end of the New Testament. Hebrews 11:1 is the Lord's definition for faith. Please write it below.

_____

_____

Read Hebrews 11 from beginning to end, expecting what I will call, a word from the Lord.

Expecting a word from God doesn't mean you will hear an audible voice, but you may read a sentence or phrase that really piques your interest. Many times the Lord will use something like this to get your undivided attention and make you curious enough to stop, look and listen to what He wants you to hear. So, if something in this passage really stands out to you, stop, write it down and spend a few minutes thinking on that. As my mother would say, "Chew on that for a while." Don't get hung up expecting a certain answer; everybody's may be different.

What was your word(s) from God as you read Hebrews 11?

_____

_____

Can you believe the incredible things God did in lives filled with faith in Him? Remember, God is the same yesterday, today and forever *(Hebrews 13:8)*. He wants to do incredible things in our life too. Jesus tells us that if we have the faith of a tiny mustard seed nothing will be impossible for us *(Matt. 17:20)*. I must confess reading Hebrews 11, there are a few verses I would love to remove. How like weak man (or woman in this case) desiring to eliminate the uncomfortable. The one thing I did not want to face ended up being my word from the Lord. I would love to pick something like Enoch and how he was taken away so that he did not see death. That is definitely my kind of story! Just pass right on over all the tough stuff and make a bee line for the good. That's not God's plan for me here; He wants me to face the difficult. Let's do that together.

Look back starting at the middle of verse 35-38. Ouch! That had to hurt. Don't get scared and run; you can rest assured this whole study is not about the hard stuff. Sometimes God has a reason for us to face something unpleasant. I believe God wants us to see the incredible faith required from men and women to die such a horrific death for Him. These were not some every day Joes that were half-hearted about their faith in God. They meant what they said. When they said they loved Jesus and He was Lord of their life, they took it to the extreme. Dying for Him or being tortured in His name is in rare cases, at least here in America, but isn't that what He really wants from each of us? No, not torture, but He wants us to take our faith to the extreme. He is asking us to be willing to live outside of the comfortable because of our faith in Him.

How does this extreme faith talk make you feel?

_____

Are you thinking, "That's not me, I'm not extreme about anything." I understand, but if God will give you the faith to live a more extreme life for Him, would you be willing to? Can you say to Him, "God, that's not me, but if you want it to be, You give me the faith to do it."? Put the ball in His court, and see what He does with it. All He needs from you is the willingness to allow Him to work.

How willing are you to give God the ball and allow Him freedom to work in your life? Check one.

_____ I'm not willing
_____ I wish I were, but I'm not
_____ I think I am willing, but unsure
_____ I am willing, but afraid
_____ I am willing and ready

If I were to guess which one you checked, I would say it was one of the last four on the willing list. I don't think you would be doing this study without, at the very least, a desire to be willing. Wherever you are, remember, we are on a quest together to grow and experience God's healing and our wholeness.

Let's crawfish back to Hebrews 11. There are three words in verse 35 that I overlooked at first, but the Lord did not let me completely miss it. The words are, "not accepting deliverance." Is that saying deliverance was there for them had they chosen to accept it? I think it does. They had their eyes set on the joy that was set before them (Hebrews 12:2). They were looking beyond the moment and the pain. They weren't caught up in their suffering but were expecting to receive something in heaven they could not fathom here on earth. God gave them all they needed, to do what they had chosen to do.

One last point – if they had the faith to be able to choose being tortured for their faith, do you think that their faith would have fallen short in their deliverance had they chosen deliverance instead? I won't answer; it's your turn.

_____

_____

If that scares you, it's okay, just be honest. It scares the daylights out of me!

What do you desperately need God to do or change in your life?

_____

Let the words of Mark 9:23 be written on the tablet of your heart, memorize them, and think about how that truth can make a difference in the situation you have written above.

Today's Memory Verse:
MARK 9: 23
Jesus said to him, "If you can believe, all things are possible to him who believes."

DAY 2: FAITH & HOPE

Do you remember God's definition of faith?
HEBREWS 11:1
Now faith is the substance of things hoped for, the evidence of things not seen.

What are we hoping for?
2nd Corinthians 5:7 tells us "… *we walk by faith, not by sight.*" In other words, we are steadfastly walking in what we hope for

and not yet able to see. Jesus said, *"Blessed are those who have not seen and yet believed."(John 20:29)* Let's talk about what we are hoping for. Each one of us could say we have hoped for something that really did not mean much in the big picture. Maybe we have hoped for leather seats in a new car, a steak rather than chicken for dinner, or the perfect jeans to wear on a date. Nothing wrong with that, but then life happens. Things get tough, and what we drive, eat, and wear become a trivial matter and a distant memory. There are seasons of life when things seem to go from bad to worse.

Do you have a situation that appears hopeless? Is it the same need you wrote about yesterday or another? Whatever it is; please write it down.

I have good news. Hopeless and desperate times are when the Lord likes to show up. When you have exhausted every resource, when everyone (mostly the wise of this earth) has declared nothing can be done, it is over, impossible, too late, etc... The words spoken to you about your situation may be different from these, but you know what they are. They may be playing over and over again like a recording in your mind. If so, push the stop button, take out the CD, and replace it with another.

Write down any words of hopelessness that haunt your mind about your situation.

Now is commitment time. Whenever these words come back to your mind, reject them and replace them by speaking (not thinking, speaking – We'll talk about this further into the study.) Jesus' words (underlined) in Matthew 19:26 instead.

MATTHEW 19:26
But Jesus looked at them and said to them,
"With men this is impossible, but with God all things are possible."

EPHESIANS 2:12
That at that time you were without Christ being aliens from the commonwealth of Israel and strangers from the covenant of promises, having no hope and without God in the world.

In your seemingly hopeless situation,
what are you hoping for?

_____

_____

According to Ephesians 2:12, at what point in life would we ever find ourselves without hope? Check each answer that applies.

_____ without Jesus as our Lord and Savior

_____ trying to live through desperate circumstances on our own

_____ knowing Jesus as Lord and Savior yet abandoned by those we love with no home, food, or money

My point is: in Christ, we will never be without hope.

Read Jeremiah 32:17.

What is too hard for God?

_____

PSALM 42:11
Why art thou cast down, O my soul?
And why art thou disquieted within me?
Hope thou in God:
For I shall yet praise him,
who is the health of my countenance, and my God

Jesus is our hope. He is the Resurrection and the Life. He is our joy, peace, refuge, shelter, provider, strength, and the list goes on and on. However, we are looking to Jesus as our healer, the Healer, and we are placing our hope in the Truth of God's Word.) Psalm 103:3 tells us the Lord *"heals all your diseases"* and Psalm 147:3

states, *"He heals the brokenhearted and binds up their wounds."* Let the words of 1 Peter 5:7 encourage you before we move on.

1ST PETER 5:7
"casting all your care upon Him, for He cares for you."

An old hymn is playing through my mind:
"Oh how He loves you and me,
Oh how He loves you and me,
He gave His life,

What more could He give,
Oh how He loves you,
Oh how He loves me,
Oh how He loves you and me." [1]

How do the words of this song and today's Scriptures make you feel in terms of hope? Mark on the scale of 1-10 your response, with 1 being neutral and 10 being full of hope.

Neutral   Hope-full
1   2   3   4   5   6   7   8   9   10

Do you need healing? Is it a broken heart, a broken body, a broken marriage, broken finances, etc...? Don't let my questions limit your answers. If you have something that needs fixin', write it down.

_____

_____

As you memorize Psalm 39:7, be attentive to hope's position. We may hope for something to come to pass, but our hope is in a Who not a what; the person of Jesus Christ our Lord.

Today's Memory Verse:
PSALM 39:7
And now, Lord, what do I wait for? My hope is in You.

———————— ❊ ❀ ❊ ————————

Day 3: Faith Not Fear
Mark 5:36
As soon as Jesus heard the word that was spoken,
He said to the ruler of the synagogue,
"Do not be afraid; only believe."

Imagine, you've just been told your daughter has a brain tumor. This is the child who comes to you and no one else to kiss her seen or unseen bo-bos, the only one who laughs at your corny jokes. What registers in your mind? Terror. Fear grips your body. A wave of nausea engulfs you. Your throat constricts. You can't breathe. The compassionate yet grim looking doctor says she has 3 months to live, so make the best of it. Jesus first words to us are, "Do not be afraid; only believe." Oh yeah right! These words seem like another part of the horror. How can you not be afraid at a time like this? Jesus tells us how, "only believe." If He is going to do what He alone can do, there is no room for fear or unbelief. Let's look at Dr. Luke's account of a similar impossible situation.

Read Luke 8:49-56 and fill in the blanks below.
What does Jesus add to, "Do not be afraid, only believe…"? **(vs.50)**

_____

What did those weeping do when Jesus told them not to weep because she was asleep? (vs.53)

_____

They ridiculed because they knew she was_____.
(vs. 53)

What did Jesus do next? (vs. 54)

_____

16

There was no room for fear or unbelief. I have heard it said fear is like faith turned inside out and gives more power to what we are afraid of than to the Lord. Jesus sent all with that problem outside. Sometimes the facts hurt us; the fact is, she was dead, and they knew it. Facts do not matter to Jesus because He sees with eyes of a different nature. If we look at everything in life through our physical eyes and hear only with our physical ears, our life will be filled with heartache and despair. In the words of Jesus, *"be of good cheer."*

JOHN 16:33
"These things I have spoken to you, that in Me you may have peace. In the world you will have tribulation; but be of good cheer, I have overcome the world."

Have you ever experienced something that caused fear to be the ruling factor in your mind? If so, what?

_____

How was fear a hindrance?

_____

We will have difficult times in this world. That's a definite. The question is, what are we going to do when they come? Are we going to be fearful or faithful?

Read Romans 8:35-39
What can separate you from the love of Christ?

_____

After studying today's lesson what does this mean to you?

_____

My dear sister in Christ, "only believe;" our God has promised us the victory!

Today's Memory Verse:
1ST CORINTHIANS 15:57
But thanks be to God, who gives us the victory, through our Lord Jesus Christ.

———————— ❈ ᘓ ❧ ————————

DAY 4: JOY REVEALS FAITH

PROVERBS 17:22
A merry heart does good, like medicine,
but a broken spirit dries the bones.

"I got the joy, joy, joy, joy down in my heart,
down in my heart, down in my heart.
I got the joy, joy, joy, joy down in my heart,
down in my heart to stay.

And if the devil doesn't like it he can
sit on a tack (Ouch!),
sit on a tack (Ouch!),
sit on a tack (Ouch!),
and if the devil doesn't like it he can sit on a tack,
sit on a tack today!" [2]

Do you recognize this song? This memory of Vacation Bible School is embedded in my mind. Studying about joy I realized there is much more to this childhood song than I ever thought before. The enemy does not like us to have joy in our heart. He loathes joy more than I do beets. Look back at Proverbs 17:22 at the beginning of today's lesson. The word, medicine, in the original Hebrew language means healing or a cure. A heart filled with gladness and joy is God's prescription for healing. Nehemiah 8:10 says that the joy of the Lord is your strength.

Read Isaiah 12:2-3 and fill in the blanks.
_____ is my salvation.
I will _____, and not be _____
_____ is my strength and song.
He has also become my _____.

18

Write verse 3.

In this passage, salvation in Hebrew means; welfare, prosperity, salvation by God, and victory. Joy is the ladle, or hopefully, the bucket we use to draw water from the well of wellbeing, success, deliverance, and triumph. The question on your mind right now may be, "But how do I get joy?" King David may have your answer.

Read Psalm 16:11
Where do we find joy at its peak?

What is at the Lord's right hand?

Read Psalm 21:6
What does the Lord do for us when we come into His presence?

Read Psalm 36:7-8
What happens to those who take refuge in the Lord?

His presence is a gift and joy is the package opened. People approach opening a present in different ways; some, in their excitement, shred the paper in the blink of an eye to get to the surprise inside. Others, like myself, savor unwrapping the gift. Getting to the inner treasure, the anticipation, builds excitement and joy lingers. Your personality and needs may dictate how you desire to approach Jesus. Desperation may thrust you facedown, by-passing all but His sanctuary. Delight may gently urge you to slow down and bask in the glory that surrounds the beauty within. But one way or the other, what we need is His presence and its treasure, joy.

Joy is faith in action, and in a trial, sets our faith on center stage and glorifies God. Joy exceeds offense and pain. Are your circumstances too painful to wade through to find anything rejoice worthy? Rejoice in Christ, who He is and all that He has done for you. Sometimes we must retrace our steps into the past and retrieve the morsels we dropped along the path to rediscover our present something to sing about.

PSALM 98:1
Oh sing to the LORD a new song! For he has done marvelous things, for His right hand and His holy arm have gained Him the victory.

Tell about a time you experienced God's presence in the midst of hard times and because of His presence you were able to rejoice.

_____

_____

Remembering God's past work builds our joy muscles. Here is another joy building exercise. Find a quite place, take your Bible, and tell God that you need to know the richness of His joy in your life. Tell Him you need Him and desire to live joyful. Read Psalms. I have selected a few personal favorites. Read until you realize His presence and let Him fill you up.

Joy building Scriptures: Psalm 27, 46, or 91 (read one or read them all)

Which Psalm did you read?_____

How did God reveal Himself to you during this spiritual exercise?

_____

_____

Romans 15:13 is my prayer for you. Let it be your prayer for you.

Today's Memory Verse:
ROMANS 15:13
Now may the God of hope fill you with all joy and peace in believing, that you may abound in hope by the power of the Holy Spirit.

──────────── *❀* ────────────

DAY 5: MORE FAITH

PSALM 115:14
May the Lord give you increase more and more,
you and your children.

Congratulations! You are about to complete your first week of your journey. I pray your faith is growing and will grow further than you ever imagined.

EPHESIANS 3:20
Now to Him who is able to do exceedingly abundantly above all that
we ask or think, according to the power that works in us.

Let's summarize where we've been this week studying faith.
Day 1 – God uses ordinary people willing to live by faith in Him.
Day 2 – With our faith in Christ, we are never without hope.
Day 3 – Faith leaves no room for fear, only believing.
Day 4 – God gives joy in His presence, and joy reveals our faith.

Today's lesson focuses on how we have faith and ultimately get more by looking at two important faith factors highlighted in the book of Romans. First, *Romans 10:17* states, *"So then faith comes by hearing, and hearing by the word of God."* We must never under estimate the inherent ability of God's word to add to our faith. Our faith is fed and nourished by His word, just as our physical bodies are fed and nourished by veggies, bread, and water. For some of us, it may be more like meat, potatoes, and Coca-Cola! *Romans 12:3* tells us God gives each believer in Christ *"a measure of faith."* If Jesus is your Lord and Savior, you have faith, and God gave it to you.

JAMES 1:17
Every good gift and every perfect gift is from above,
and comes down from the father of lights,
with whom there is no variation or shadow of turning.

Good gifts comes from God and He gives gifts to His children custom made for each one. The Lord intimately knows us. *(Psalm 139:1)* He has counted the number of hairs on our head *(Luke12:7)* and knows our words before they ever make it to our mouth *(Psalm 139:4)*. Yikes! That can be down right scary knowing some of the thoughts that pass through my mind. But let us not forget that His mercy endures forever. Thank You Jesus! Yesterday we saw joy as a gift given by God, and today we see that faith is a gift. Actually faith is the first gift in relationship with God and would not exist without Him. But do we have all we can ever have?

Do you need an increase of faith? _____

Read Luke 17:5
Who is talking to Jesus? _____

What do they ask Him for? _____

I'm thinking if the apostles needed an increase in faith, we most certainly could use more. They asked for more, and we can too. Ask God to increase your faith; this is His desire. How do I know? *Hebrews 11:6* says *"faith pleases Him."* Why would He hold something back that pleases Him? Okay, so you need one more reason.

Turn to Luke 11: 9-13 and read it out loud. You need to hear this! Remember our first point? Faith comes by hearing God's word. In your own words summarize what you read.

_____

_____

I know everyone reading this will not be able to relate to having an earthly father whose name was in the dictionary as the definition to daddy, but my daddy's was. Now in heaven with Jesus, I'm sure he is having a blast (Knowing Daddy, He's probably sitting by the river Jordan with a fishing pole). Daddy would do anything in his power for me and gave me whatever I wanted that he could afford and wouldn't harm me. He was the greatest! But even he could not compare to our heavenly Daddy who gives perfect gifts, gifts of faith and joy. Daddy gave gifts because of the relationship we had. Next week, we will sew our study together with the binding thread of relationship. I am proud of you and look forward to another week together.

Our memory verse repeats today's valuable lesson, reminding us that we can and should, ask for an increase in faith.

Today's Memory Verse:
LUKE 17:5
And the apostles said to the Lord, "Increase our faith."

Be Blessed!

QUEST JOURNAL

Use this section as a reflection of your journey with God or write your prayer about where you've been and where you're going next.

_____

_____

_____

_____

_____

_____

_____

_____

_____

_____

_____

_____

_____

_____

_____

_____

_____

_____

_____

_____

_____

_____

_____

_____

_____

_____

_____

_____

_____

_____

_____

Week 2
It's All In The Asking

This week's goal is to finish with the understanding that asking matters to God because asking means relationship. Relationship with God is the underlying tone in these next five days. So I am asking you to keep the word, "relationship" on the forefront of your mind each day.

DAY 1: ASK FOR WHAT?

JAMES 4:2-3
You lust and do not have.
You murder and covet and cannot obtain. You fight and war.
Yet you do not have because you do not ask.
You ask and do not receive,
because you ask amiss,
that you may spend it on your own pleasures.

You would not believe the things I've asked from God. I have asked for the perfect outfit, which way to go to get to work on time, and for Him to change a person getting on my last nerve. The last one is not one you want to ask. I have yet to come to Him with the request He change another that I haven't been made aware of His call for me to be likewise changed. I have been in this place so many times it is almost comical that I am such a slow learner. God also has a grand sense of humor and at times expresses that through answering our self-centered prayers with a, "Why yes, of course, my child."

Before my husband and I got married, he said he always prayed he would be surrounded by women. He now lives in a house with a wife, three children, one dog, and two cats, all of which are female. He is living out his dream. With a grin and a wink, he is quick to say, "Be careful what you ask for; you might get it!"

Have you ever asked God for something and gotten it? If so what?

_____

Last week, Day 5, we asked God for an increase in faith. Today we look at what else we can ask God for. Please remember that faith in Jesus is the prerequisite. Before we get going, ask God to speak to you through His word.

Look up the following Scriptures and list what each says we can ask God for.

Mark 11:24 _____

John 14:13 _____

John 15:7 _____

John16:23 _____

1 John 3:22 _____

1 John 5:15 _____

Meditate on this. Tomorrow we will dig further into the concept of asking God for "whatever."

What is the word from this week's introduction that I asked you to keep on the forefront of your mind?

_____

_____

Finish today's lesson by writing out your prayer asking God for your "whatever."

_____

_____

_____

_____

Today's Memory Verse:
1ˢᵀ JOHN 5:14
And this is the confidence that we have in Him, that if we ask anything according to His will, He will hear us.

———————————— ❋ ⚏ ❋ ————————————

DAY 2: HOW DO WE ASK?

EPHESIANS 2:18
For through Him we both have access by one Spirit to the Father.

We have access to the Father, an open door invitation. So how are we going to approach Him?

Read Hebrews 10:19:23
According to verse 19, how do we enter His holy presence?

_____

_____

How do we have boldness? (vs. 19)

_____

I remember as a little girl and into my teens hearing the loud mud tires on daddy's truck when he drove into the driveway. I would run from my room to meet him as he walked in the door, throwing my arms and legs around him and giving him as big of a hug and kiss as I could. I did that boldly! I remember sitting in his lap when I was way too big to fit (we're talking as an adult). I would tell him how much I loved him and ask how much he loved me. He would stretch his arms wide, measure out a large chunk of air space, and say, "I love you this much."

I adored my Daddy, and he adored me. I knew how to get what I wanted and more, because of the love that we shared. If I needed $20.00, I boldly asked him for it while batting my eyes sweetly. The funny thing is, he knew I was putting on the charm to get what I wanted and honestly I think he loved that too. He did not mind because he knew I loved him with all of my heart. Inevitably Daddy would pull out His wallet and hand me double of what I asked for. When I asked for $20, I usually got $40. Our heavenly Daddy loves us so much and has so much more to give.

This story should have reminded you of the word we are keeping before us this week.

Please write that word._____

_____

Read 2 Corinthians 5:21

How do we become the righteousness of God?

_____

_____

_____

Read Philippians 3:9

Whose righteousness do we have?

_____

_____

By what means do we obtain this righteousness?

_____

_____

1 JOHN 3:1 *(my favorite verse)*
Behold what manner of love the Father has bestowed on us,
that we should be called children of God.

Read John 15:5 and fill in the blank.
"… for without me you can do_____."

Take a moment to glance over the questions you answered, put the Scriptures we studied together, and give your understanding of what we have and how we have it?

_____

_____

_____

_____

_____

_____

I did not have you look up anything specifically about humility; however, the lesson is an indirect approach to the subject of humility. Now it's time to answer the question: "How do we ask?" Boldly? Yes. Humbly? Absolutely! We ask humbly and boldly. I had a hard time with this in the past. For me understanding each separately wasn't a problem. The problem came joining the two. How could I be humble and groveling saying, "Lord, I'm so unworthy," and at the same time boldly come to Him saying, "I am the righteousness of God"? My problem was; I thought to be humble I had to be groveling. After looking at all of these Scriptures it should be clear why we must take a stand of humility as we boldly enter to talk with our heavenly Daddy. Because. It has absolutely, positively, nothing to do with us. We have been given the right to a high place of honor; children of the King of Kings. We respect and honor how great and powerful our heavenly Daddy is, but He is our Daddy none the less. Don't forget, it's not by anything that we have or by who we are apart from the blood of Jesus.

Today's Memory Verse:

1ST PETER 5:6

Therefore humble yourselves under the mighty hand of God, that He may exalt you in due time.

DAY 3: ASK BELIEVING

MARK 11:23
For assuredly, I say to you, whoever says to this mountain,
'Be removed and be cast into the sea,'
and does not doubt in his heart,
but believes that those things he says will be done,
he will have whatever he says.

This lesson may hurt a little, but better yet, it may help a lot. To receive full benefits from today's lesson I ask you to be up close and personal with yourself. Don't cheat yourself by allowing the discomfort of honesty to keep you from facing reality and sweeping the truth under the rug saying, "No one will ever see this or know anyway." That is all the more reason to be hard core honest. John 8:32 is a reminder of the power of truth.

JOHN 8:32
And you shall know the truth and the truth shall set you free.

The word "whatever" encompasses a wide terrain. Unlike the "whosoever" in John 3:16 which has no conditions, the "whatever" in this context does have criteria to be met. God's love is there for us no matter what, but God's blessing and favor on our life, more times than not requires a certain standard from us. Mark 11:23 (at the beginning of the lesson) gives us three points for seeing our "whatever" come to pass: 1) No doubt, 2) Believe, 3) Speak it.

Point number 1: No doubt

James 1:6-7 says that the doubter *"is like a wave of the sea driven and tossed by the wind ... a double-minded man, unstable in all his ways"*. I wonder if God thinks, "Would you make up your mind, do you want it or not?" Or even worse, "Do you believe I am who I say I am and I can do what I say I can do or not?"

Is there a place in your life that you have doubt and need to confess it?

_____

_____

Point number 2: Believe

We are going to skip over this point today and give the topic the attention it deserves on Week 4 and Week 5.

Point number 3: The "asker" must speak it.

Look back and read Mark 11:23 at the beginning of today's lesson circling the word, says, every time your read it.

Read 2 Corinthians 4:13

What does this verse say we do when we believe?

_____

_____

Proverbs 18:21 says *"death and life are in the power of the tongue."* Are your words killing what you're asking for, or, are they breathing life into the situation you need changed? Do you speak about it as though it were or do you say, "Nothing good ever happens to me?" Your words make a difference! They matter to God. He is listening to what you're saying and it affects what He is doing! God has always listened to His people and has even allowed them the awesome privilege of persuading Him to change His mind about things.

It's time to write the forefront word for this week.

_____

What words do you most commonly speak about the situation you most need changed?

_____

_____

How can you improve what you are speaking about your situation?

_____

_____

_____

Today's Memory Verse:
MATTHEW 21:22
And whatever things you <u>ask</u> in prayer, <u>believing</u>, you will receive.

DAY 4: ASK ACCORDING TO HIS WILL

1ˢᵗ JOHN 5:14
Now this is the confidence that we have in Him,
that if we ask anything according to His will, He will hear us.

Take a moment to pray. <u>Ask</u> God to penetrate His truth into your heart instilling His truth so deep nothing can remove them. Don't forget to thank Him for hearing and doing what you asked.

Dinner tonight was a refrigerator cleaning. On these evenings we are more relaxed than normal. We eat whatever and wherever. My husband and daughter were eating at the snack bar and I was in my rocking chair flipping channels while I ate my sandwich. I got up to fix myself something to drink and noticed Avery's cup was empty so I poured her some Dr. Pepper. My husband's countenance dropped; he was angry. Puzzled, I questioned him, "What's wrong?" He said, "I just got it out of my mouth that she could not have anything else to drink until she had eaten more of her food." No wonder he was mad. He thought I had deliberately gone against his word to our daughter. I apologized and took the drink from Avery until she had eaten.

The problem was I never heard him. I could not act according to his word because I did not know he had said anything. Hearing my husband was very important if I was going to act on what he desired to happen. God hearing us is important if He's going to answer our "whatevers."

What is the word that should be on the forefront of your mind?

_____

1 John 5:14 says we are to be confident that He hears us as we ask according to His will. How do we know we are asking according to His will? I thought you would never ask! We can only ask according to His will when we have come to know Him by spending time with Him. As we spend time with Him we begin to know what He wants and expects from us and for us. Tonight, I knew B.J. was angry instantly because we have spent the past fourteen years together.

My children know what I want and expect from them because they spend time with me (And I tell them whether they want to hear it or not!). They won't ask me for something they know I have forbidden. Because of our relationship, I see our likes and dislikes beginning to parallel. There are ways my children think and act as a result of living with me everyday since birth. Not all of them good because I make mistakes, but knowing Jesus every day is different. He is perfect.

The Bible is God's word to us; His love letter to His children. Scripture tells us who He is, He is like, what He approves of, how He thinks about us, and His desires and plans for us. To know Him and His ways we must spend time seeking Him through the reading of His word. His word will transform our ways and our thinking to be more like His.

Read Psalm 119:1-8 / The author used many words to describe God's word. List these words below. I started you off.

Law,
_____

_____

What benefits link up with the words listed above?

Blessed are those who walk in God's law (vs.1)
_____
_____
_____
_____
_____
_____

Read Romans 12:2

How are we transformed?
_____
_____
_____

When are we transformed?
_____
_____

Did I answer the question, "How do we know that we are asking according to His will?" If not clear, allow me the privilege to spell it out. Read your bible and you will know what is according to his will, and your prayers will be heard loud and clear!

What is your prayer you are confident He hears because it's according to His will?
_____
_____
_____
_____

Today's Memory Verse:
PSALM 34:17
The righteous cry out, and the Lord hears, and delivers them out of them all their troubles.
———————————— ❖ ⚘ ❖ ————————————

DAY 5: ASK ABIDING

JOHN 15:7
If you abide in me and my words in you,
you will ask what you desire,
and it shall be done for you.

We will pick up where we left off yesterday, but first, let's overview the week.

Day 1 – What can we ask for? Ask Whatever.
Day 2 – How do we ask? Humbly and Boldly.
Day 3 – Ask Believing and Speaking.
Day 4 – We can have whatever we ask according to His will.

What is the word we have kept before us all week?

_____

_____

How do you see relationship being a common thread throughout the daily lessons of this week?

_____

_____

On Day 4 we learned that knowing His will meant knowing His word by reading the Bible because He had His will put on paper for me and you. Today we transition to learning His will by reading the Bible to having abiding in Him and having His words in us. This is accomplished the same way, by reading the Bible. The word, abiding, has continualness at its core. Abiding reflects the daily-ness of being in His word. Sunday morning is not enough. I don't sit and talk with my husband once a week for an hour and expect him to be satisfied with that, but instead we talk before he goes to work, on the phone while he is at work, and when he gets home from work. Our communication is ongoing.

Are you getting the picture? Do you see what is ultimately important to God in the asking? Yes! You got it! Relationship.

The Creator of everything (you included), wants to hang out and talk with you! Is that not the coolest! Are you willing to give up something that might hinder you from spending time reading the Bible and abiding? Start with a commitment that you can stick with, not an unrealistic one that will have you feeling defeated after 3 days. This reminds me of the health club. I have spent most of my adult life working out, doing weights, aerobics, etc... One of the things I have watched happen time and time again is someone new coming to the gym, all pumped up to loose weight and look great, only to soon give up and go back to their old ways of eating and not exercising. Why, because they have started with an impossible goal for themselves. It might not always be impossible, but may require time and a process to reach that level of commitment.

Starting off slow and adapting to this new way of life is utmost important. If you are just starting, try giving up ten to fifteen minutes a day, television, phone, computer, for reading your Bible and talking to the Lord. You know where you are; there is always room for improvement. You decide, make the commitment, and go for it!

My commitment is to give up_____and for this amount of time_____to be spent reading and talking with the Lord.

Once your commitment is regimented into your life, then, and only then, move on. Increase your time slowly, but steadily, always growing, always moving forward, or as Paul says, *upward*. In fulfillment of *Philippians 3:14*, *"I press toward the goal for the prize of the upward call of God in Christ Jesus."*

I am proud of you for your commitment to strive for the goal of wholeness and for completing Week 2.

Today's Memory Verse:
JOHN 8:31
Then Jesus said to those Jews who believed Him, "If you abide in my word, you are my disciples indeed."

Be Blessed!

QUEST JOURNAL

Use this section as a reflection of your journey with God or write your prayer about where you've been and where you're going next.

_____

_____

_____

_____

_____

_____

_____

_____

_____

_____

_____

_____

_____

_____

_____

_____

_____

_____

_____

_____

_____

_____

_____

_____

_____

_____

_____

_____

_____

_____

_____

_____

_____

_____

_____

Week 3
Why Does God Give Us The Things We Ask?

The answer to the title question for the week is answered directly and indirectly through Scripture. During the first three days we will deal with the direct answers. At the end of the week we will turn our attention to the significance of His body and our body and how we treat them. We will not know the fulfillment of the first three days without deep consideration and appreciation of the last two. I pray you have been blessed so far and encouraged to know Him more.

DAY 1: COMMANDMENTS KEPT

1 JOHN 3: 22-23
And whatever we ask we receive from Him,
because we keep His commandments
and do these things that are pleasing in His sight.

How many times in scripture does God promise us blessing if we will only obey? Many! God blesses those who walk a holy walk.

"THE HOLY WALK"
Many see this walk as impossible, unexciting, and simply not worth it. The Holy walk is possible, extremely exciting and more worth it than anything I have ever done in my life. That comes from an ex-pleasure lover who thought life was all about me. The holy walk begins with the recognition of the holiness of God; seeing God as He really is. This positions us to desire doing something different than how we have always done things. Without knowing Christ we would never consider living a holy life, and apart from Him it would be impossible. Praise God,

that we can do all things through Christ who strengthens us, even walk a holy walk.

Why would we want to attempt this holy walk anyway? Jesus died for you and I and He would have if either of us had been the only one on the planet. That inspires me not only to love Him, but to want to please Him. How about you? When we are moved by His display of love, we will seek ways to express our love in return. Our treasures and desires change as we come to know Him better. We begin to seek the pleasure of hearing those blessed words at the end of the journey, "Well done good and faithful servant." *(Matthew 25:21)*

I can so well remember falling in love with my husband and wanting to do the things that pleased him. Cooking his favorite foods was definitely a big one. He loves to eat and is fun to cook for. He is an expressive eater and you know when he really likes what you cooked. As I fell in love with him I looked for ways to make him happy, so I could hear those blessed words, "I do!" And I did and I am glad that I did and that He did - if you know what I mean!

According to 1 John 3:22-23 at the beginning of today's lesson, what is pleasing to God?

_____

_____

Read Hebrews 11:5-6

What was Enoch's testimony before he was taken? (vs.5)

_____

_____

What pleases God? (vs.6)_____

_____

Faith and keeping the Lord's commandments are linked together, because without faith we wouldn't have the drive to do things His way. Our motivation is our faith. Our desire to please Him is because we Jesus paid the ultimate price for us to have eternal life. In John 10:10 Jesus takes it a step further than eternal life.

Read John 10:10 Why did Jesus come? Write the whole reason.

_____

_____

_____

_____

He did not die for us to live a barely getting by, feeling okay kind of life. The word abundantly in the original Greek language means exceeding abundantly, superior, extraordinary, surpassing, and uncommon. Wow! That is huge! For us to settle for less maybe an insult to the Most High God who sent His One and Only Son to give us the extraordinary and superior.

What have you been settling for that is less than extraordinary?

_____

_____

_____

_____

_____

Today's Memory Verse:
1 CORINTHIANS 2:9
But as it is written: "Eye has not seen, nor ear heard, nor have entered into the heart of man the things which God has prepared for those who love him."

————————— ❖ 🕮 ❖ —————————

DAY 2: TO GLORIFY THE FATHER THROUGH THE SON

JOHN 14:13
And whatever you ask in My name, that I will do, that the Father may be glorified.

Jesus brought His Father glory. The work He does in us and through us, also, bring the Father glory. In other words, Jesus' work in us gives the world a correct opinion of the Father. When God is glorified, people watching are going to see Him for who He really is; sovereign and omnipotent, high and lifted up, holy and righteous, and especially loving and compassionate. For lack of paper I have to stop somewhere, but you get the picture. As the apostle John said in *John 21:25, "And there are also many other things that Jesus did, which if they were written one by one, I suppose that even the world itself could not contain the books that would be written. Amen."* We have a huge God!

How does Jesus work in us to bring God glory? He accomplishes those things in us that would never happen without Him. Maybe you have tried to stop smoking so many times you have lost count, but one day you give it to Jesus and you are set free from that addiction. People see, you tell, and God gets glory. Maybe you have a fear of praying out loud. The first few years of my journey with God I was afraid of praying out loud. Now I will pray in front of and for anyone. People have seen and heard me pray and I have also told them of my past fears that Christ has overcome. God gets the glory because on my own I would never have done this.

Is there something specific in your life that you have accomplished, because you know that He somehow helped you to accomplish it? If so what?

_____

_____

_____

_____

This is your testimony of God in your life.
Tell it! That is how He gets the glory!

Have others seen or have you told?_____

_____

Only through His Holy Spirit living and working in and through us can He be glorified. *Psalm 96:8* tells us, *"Give to the Lord the glory due His name; bring an offering and come into His courts."* How?

ROMANS 12:1
... I beseech you therefore, brethren, by the mercies of God,
that you present your bodies a living sacrifice,
Holy, and acceptable to God,
which is your reasonable service.

Let's not overlook the invitation to enter into His courts. Psalm 100 says we enter His gates with thanksgiving and into His courts with praise. When God works in our life and we recognize it, we can not contain our praises to Him. That must be where Jesus got the statement about stones crying out. Someone or something is going to praise Him or bust.

List some ways you can give God the glory due Him in your life.

_____

_____

_____

_____

I pray you had a light bulb moment today about the impossibility of glorifying God without Him at work in your life. He is the only one able to accomplish anything of lasting or eternal value in our lives.

Today's Memory Verse:
COLOSSIANS 3:17
And whatever you do in word or deed, do all in the name of the Lord Jesus, giving thanks to God the Father through Him.

DAY 3: THAT OUR JOY MAY BE FULL

JOHN 16:24
Until now you have asked nothing in my name.
Ask and you will receive, that your joy may be full.

How like a perfect Daddy to want His child to be happy and full of joy. John 16:24 knocks out the image I once had. I saw God as a stern disciplinarian that I would never be good enough to please and who wanted me to give up everything and have no fun. I was looking through unfocused lens; my vision was blurry. He likes to give us what we ask that we will be full of joy. God wants us to be happy. He is not sitting up in Heaven slapping us on the back of our hand every time we ask for something saying, "No, No, No!" But instead, He is saying, "Would you please ask me? I want to give, and I want you to be full of joy."

Jesus was rebuked by the Pharisees for being a partying man. He was simply having too much fun. They were sure he was a sinful man having all that fun! They were so set in their ways, rituals, and laws that they could not have fun and thought anyone that did was wrong; yes, even evil. If someone tells you being a Christian isn't fun, they evidently aren't hanging out with Jesus because He is loads of fun and the more you hang out with Him the more fun He is! They might be hanging out with other people who call themselves Christians yet really aren't hanging out with Jesus either. Maybe they are like the Pharisees, doing all the right things and walking all around Jesus and never realizing who He is.

Have you ever experienced joy in a relationship with Jesus?

_____

_____

If not, what image do you have of the Lord that may be holding you back?

_____

_____

We talked about the holy walk on Day 1 this week. The excitement of the holy walk comes from removing the static. We need clear reception on the "God and me" station. Focusing our attention on the Lord and letting go of the world and its enticements, our past, or anything that takes our focus off God removes the static. The more we let go, the more we hear from Him. Not because He wasn't talking before, but because there was too much static. We could pick up bits and pieces and that only led to frustration and confusion. There are times we are desperate to know His answer. The thrill is God speaking loud and clear. By this, I don't mean audible, but knowing deep in your heart and mind that He has given you the answer He wanted you to have. Walking on a cloud will be an understatement when you realize your heavenly Daddy, the Most High God, the Creator of everything, just gave you the perfect answer. He can give no less than the perfect answer, and knows everything about everything. Talk about the ultimate counselor! As we walk with Him day by day He reveals His worth. There is nothing and no one who can compare to his matchless worth! Praise his holy name!

What influence, that you can control, can you say may be causing your "God and Me" station to be altered by static? (PLEASE BE HONEST!)

_____

_____

_____

_____

Today's Memory Verse:
PSALM 16:11
You will show me the path of life; in Your presence is fullness of joy; at Your right hand are pleasures forevermore.

———————— ✣ ❦ ✣ ————————

DAY 4: BLOOD COVENANT

HEBREWS 9:22
*And according to the law almost all things are purified with blood,
and without shedding of blood there is no remission.*

Read John 1:29

What does John the Baptist call Jesus?

_____

_____

What does John the Baptist say the Lamb of God takes away?

_____

_____

Read Rev. 5:1-14 and answer these questions:

Who was slain? (vs.6)

_____

Who alone is found worthy? (vs. 9 &12)

_____

Saints sing a new song to the Lamb.
What do they sing is the reason for His worthiness? (vs.9)

_____

_____

Jesus, the Lamb of God, took away the sins of the world. He
is the only One who could and would. Jesus, the only One who
should not, did. Worthy is the Lamb!

Read 1 Corinthians 11:23-32

Verse 29 says that we judge ourselves if we take the bread and
the cup in an unworthy manner, not discerning the Lord's body.
The word discerning in the original Greek language means to

separate, make a distinction, discriminate, or to prefer. Christ is separate and distinct. There is none like Him. We should discriminate and prefer Him.

Write out 1 Corinthians 11:30

_____

_____

HEBREWS 10:29
Of how much worse punishment, do you suppose, will he be thought worthy who has trampled the Son of God underfoot, counted the blood of the covenant by which he was sanctified a common thing, and insulted the Spirit of grace?

Theses are strong words. My mother would say, "That's a hard one to swallow."

Christ is no common thing! His blood, His covenant, His grace are not ordinary, but instead, a treasure, a rare jewel. It can be dangerous, and even deadly, if we don't make the distinction. I am overwhelmed with a realization that we must seek Him to keep us from this serious offense of not recognizing His holiness, majesty, glory, grace, mercy, and His love.

Voice the prayer below aloud.

Precious Savior and Lord,
May it not be that I would ever overlook the distinction of who You are and what You did for me. Lord, keep me from ever becoming hard-hearted to the fact that Your body was broken and Your blood poured out for me. Please make my heart more tender to Who You are each and every day. In the holy name of Jesus I pray. Amen.

Today's Memory Verse:
EPHESIANS 1:7
In Him we have redemption through His blood, the forgiveness of sins, according to the riches of His grace.

─────────── ❖{ ☙ }❖ ───────────

DAY 5: HOLY TEMPLE

1 CORINTHIANS 3:16
Do you not know that you are the temple of God
and that the Spirit of God dwells in you?

Have you ever brought someone to church who did not know
and reverence Jesus and before they left the sanctuary they said
a curse word? Well, I have. It took my breath away. How could
they stand in God's house and say that? In reality, the church
building is a place where believers gather to worship Him, not His
dwelling place. Yes, He is there because we are there worshipping
and praising Him. Yet still, it is not His address. During the Old
Testament days, God did choose to dwell in a structure. The new
covenant changed that and the Lord has a new address, the body
of individuals who trust Him as Lord and Savior.

What a responsibility to keep His home clean and pure! Think
about it. He is a holy, righteous, and perfect God. If we would
want to keep our churches clean how much more our bodies.

Look at it this way. The Queen of England or the President of
the United States gives you a call. They are coming to your house!
Would you do anything to make it more presentable? Would you
leave dirty dishes in the sink, the garbage can overflowing, hair
around the bathroom sink, and clothes on the floor? Please tell
me you would clean it up! I know I would be in a frenzy to make
it as perfect as possible. The King of Kings and Lord of Lords
lives in us. What do we fill our bodies with?
Let's look at what God has to say about our bodies and
what we should do or not do with them.

What does Psalm 101:3 have to say about our eyes?

_____

_____

Read 2 Corinthians 6:14-7:1

What does verse 17 say about what we touch?

_____

_____

Read 1 Corinthians 6:12-20

Verse 13 states that the body is not for sexual immorality, but for

_____

_____

What reason does verse 18 give about sexual immorality being different from other sins?

_____

_____

1 THESSALONIANS 4:7-8
For God did not call us to uncleanness, but in holiness.
Therefore he who rejects this does not reject man,
but God who has also given us His Holy Spirit.

Please don't think God's Word is talking about legalism. Holiness is not legalism; or laws or a formula. Holiness is purification in progress. This goes back to relationship. It's about walking with Him. In so doing He reveals to each believer what He considers to be a holy walk, and He places the conviction on our heart as we go. Our job is to respond and make the move toward holiness as He reveals what He expects.

As you read the scriptures today did anything come to your mind or pierce your heart? Could God be calling you to the next step in your purification? If so, write it down and ask God to give you the grace and strength you need to do His will.

_____

_____

_____
_____
_____
_____
_____
_____
_____
_____
_____

Today's Memory Verse:
2 CORINTHIANS 7:1

Therefore, having these promises, beloved, let us cleanse ourselves from all filthiness of the flesh and spirit, perfecting holiness in the fear of God.

Be Blessed!

QUEST JOURNAL

Use this section as a reflection of your journey with God or write your prayer about where you've been and where you're going next.

_____

_____

_____

_____

_____

_____

_____

_____

_____

_____

_____

_____

_____

_____

_____

_____

_____

_____

_____

_____

_____

_____

_____

_____

_____

_____

_____

_____

_____

_____

_____

Week 4
Actions to Healing

The Bible gives us actions to take to experience healing. Maybe your healing will take everything listed and maybe God will do it with only one act of faith, or maybe He will just do it. One thing is for sure He can do what He says He can do. The Lord is able!

DAY 1: AND BELIEVE!

JOHN 14:12
Most Assuredly, I say to you he who believes in Me,
the works that I do He will do also;
and greater works than these he will do,
because I go to My Father.

"And believe" is a component of the equation that is a must for wholeness. This week each day will have a specific active instruction, steps of faith, from the Word of God, but will have no value without the "and believe." Faith is believing. God is looking for those who say, "I believe."

Flip back in you workbook to Week 2, Day 3. This question below is extracted from point # 3 please rewrite the answer.

What does this verse say we do when we believe?

_____

_____

Read Matthew 13:53-58

What did the people of Jesus home town miss out on because of unbelief? (vs.58)

_____

_____

Does verse 58 just blow you over? I had to let it soak in for a minute.

How like our Christian walk. Jesus healed all who came to him in one place. *"But when Jesus knew it, He withdrew Himself from there. And great multitudes followed Him, and He healed them all." (Matt.12:15)* Yet one chapter over, and a few parables later He is healing, but not everyone. Unbelief had gotten in the way. Is that happening today, we see someone healed, but more times than not, it seems Jesus is overlooking many broken lives. Are we to blame or is He? Check out Jesus' words in Matt. 14:31, *"O you of little faith, why did you doubt?"* I wonder if there is a touch of sadness in the voice of the God-Man.

On the other hand - You did not think I would let you off so easily, now did you?

Read James 2:17-20 and fill in the blanks below.

Even the _____ believe and _____ .(vs.19)

Faith without works is _____ , being alone. (vs.20)

The point is: the Lord is not letting us off the hook just because we say we believe. Faith and works go hand in hand. You can't have one without the other. Well, I guess you can, but let's just say it is not a good thing, or better yet, it is not a God thing. Our actions will display what we truly believe.

What do you need God to do in your life?

_____

_____

Now take a moment to think about and write down what you really believe about this need.

_____

_____

_____

_____

Today's Memory Verse:
PSALM 27:13
I would have lost heart, unless I had believed that I would see the goodness of the Lord in the land of the living.

⁌ 🕮 ⁍

DAY 2: MAKE A CHOICE AND BELIEVE

1 JOHN 5:5
Who is he who overcomes the world,
but he who believes that Jesus is the Son of God?

You have a choice to make when faced with any trial or affliction in your life. Fear or faith, doubt or belief; it's a choice to either stand strong in the Lord or to fall prey to the enemy. These decisions, we make daily whether things are going great or not.

In Joshua 24:15, Joshua proclaims to the people of Israel to choose for themselves whom they will serve and then boldly professes, *"But as for me and my house, we will serve the Lord."* Living for the Lord is a daily choice; it does not come natural to us. What does comes natural is to serve ourselves, to do what we like, or what feels good, or what makes us happy. If we fall into the it's all about me trap, we are choosing, and that choice is not to serve God.

I hope through this study you are choosing to have your Bible with you as we discuss the Scriptures. This gives God the opportunity to speak to you in a very personal and intimate way. I don't want you to miss out on a very special blessing. But, it is your choice.

Read Romans 8:8 and Galatians 5:16-18.

Answer the questions according to these scriptures

Is there anything good in our flesh? _____
The flesh and the Spirit, do they ever agree? _____
How can we overrule the flesh? _____

Read Deut. 30:11-20.

Please read it out loud, and remember there's power in the spoken word of God.

PSALM 29:4
The voice of the Lord is powerful;
the voice of the Lord is full of majesty.

Is there anything that struck you as significant or that you kept going back to as you read the passage from Deuteronomy? If so, what do you think God was saying to you through that?

_____
_____
_____
_____

God gave us the freedom to make our own choices and then rewards us for choosing Him. I love Him! He thrills me to my toes!

Today's Memory Verse:
PSALM 1:6
For the Lord knows the way of the righteous, but the way of the ungodly shall perish.

———————————— ❋ ❦ ❊ ———————————

DAY 3: CRY OUT AND BELIEVE

PSALM 107:19-20
Then they cried out to the Lord in their trouble,
and He saved them out of their distresses.
He sent His word and healed them,
and delivered them from their distresses.

Grab your Bible. We're starting the day running.

Read Matthew 9:27-30

Who was following Jesus? _____
What did Jesus do for them? _____

    These two men were not easily deterred from their pursuit of Jesus. The story tells us that while they followed Him, they were crying out to Him for mercy. The original word here for crying in Greek is "krazo." Does that remind you of the word from the English language, crazy? The word "krazo" means to scream, shriek, or exclaim. Do you get a picture of two crazy blind men following Him down the road screaming and pleading with Him for mercy? They were not too proud to beg and had thrown any care of what others thought of them to the wind. All that mattered to them was one thing; sight. They wanted to be healed. And they knew that He was the One who could do it, if only He would. They did what they knew to do; beg loudly and persistently.

What question did Jesus ask them? _____
_____
_____

Do you think Jesus knew they believed He could heal their sight?
_____

Of course He knew they believed after that big display. But He says that if we confess Him before men, He will confess us before the angels and he who denies Him before man will be denied before the angels. Their confession, *"Yes Lord."* mattered. Then touching their eyes, He says, *"According to your faith let it be to you."* And their eyes were opened.

Mark 5:1-20 has another story of a man crying out (same word, "krazo") This man is the demon-possessed man that was living in the cemetery. The men in the two Scripture passages we read today have different types of problems, in need of different types of healing, but each situation appears hopeless. There is another common thread that binds them together. These people are "krazo". They are desperate. They have nothing to lose and everything to gain if Jesus will come through for them because, no doubt, they believe He can. But will He? Glory to God, He does!

What are you desperate for? _____

_____

Are you desperate enough that you are "krazo", willing to throw caution, reputation, all pride to the wind and cry out to the One who can, "Will You have mercy on me, Lord?" His next question to you will be, "Do you believe that I am able?" Speak it. Confess it. Tell Him you believe. And if you doubt, pray, *"Lord, I believe, help my unbelief"* as the father did in *Mark 9:24* who didn't want unbelief to get in the way of His son's healing.

Today's Memory Verse:
PSALM 30:2
Oh Lord my God, I cried out to You, and You healed me.

───────────── ❈ ⚬ ❈ ─────────────

Day 4: Speak Out And Believe

Luke 6:45
*A good man out of the good treasure
of his heart brings forth good;
and an evil man out of the evil treasure
of his heart brings forth evil.
For out of the abundance of the heart his mouth speaks.*

This lesson gets me going! I am so passionate about this message; its part of my heart's cry for the Lord. All I can say to you is "bear with me" (pun intended). You will get this in just a few minutes.

"The Blessing of the Holy Talk"

What is "Holy Talk"? Could it be speaking the living and powerful word of God? I can testify to the fact that as I began to test the word of God out by speaking it aloud into different facets of my life, even I thought I sounded like a freak. I found it awkward to speak in ways so different than what I was accustomed to. One reason for the awkwardness was because it's so different from the way most people are speaking. As time went on I began to feel less freaky, but to the world I probably still sound a little weird. But have you listened to the world lately?

Are we to live less than an abundant life because we are concerned the world thinks we sound a little different? The answer is an emphatic, "NO!" They are dying for it and don't know it. They want something different. They want something that will make a difference in the circumstances of their life. The problem has been, we as Christians have been too afraid to be different. Why? Because we might suffer a little persecution, someone might make fun of us, or talk about us. So what! Would we limit our life to that?

Read 2 Kings 2:23 & 24

What happened when Elisha (God's man) was made fun of?

_____

_____

What did Elisha do?

_____

_____

What happened to His offenders?

_____

_____

   Does that make you feel like dancing and singing, "Can't Touch This!"? (I hope your not so young you can't remember the MC Hammer song.) There will always be someone somewhere who will find something about you to talk about. That's what my mother always says and I have come to the knowledge that she is much wiser than I once gave her credit for (When I was 15 I thought she was just plain dumb.). If people will talk about you anyway, for one reason or another, why not give them something to talk about that will make a difference in your life and the kingdom of God. They will notice the blessing God is pouring out on your life because the power of His word is changing situations and circumstances in your favor. They will see that different does not necessarily mean bad. They might even see that God's different actually means good.

   And there you are, your life and your words are a testimony to the good things of God and to the good things He has in store for those who walk the walk and talk the talk. To this moment I can see, but little cost and great rewards for being different for the sake of my Lord and Savior. I am praying for you that you will not miss the valuable life changing treasures in this lesson on the words that we speak.

Ask God to pierce your heart with the truth of His words.

Now read Proverbs 12:18.
If you were pierced with a sword what would that do to you? (from the least to the worst case scenerio) _____

_____

_____

_____

_____

What does this scripture say that the tongue of the wise does?

_____

_____

Today's Memory Verse:
PSALM 34:15
The eyes of the Lord are on the righteous, and His ears are open to their cry.

You're doing great! Hang in there!

DAY 5: SPEAK OUT AND BELIEVE (PART 2)

MATTHEW 13:36
But I say to you that for every idle word men may speak,
they will give account of it in the day of judgment.

I had a feeling this might take a while, but what valuable missed treasures in God's Word. I say they're missed because I don't hear His people speaking God's Word over their life enough. This is a significant part of our strength and power to overcome "whatever." Yesterday we learned the tongue of the wise promotes health, but used negatively or wrongly can pierce us like a sword.

PROVERBS 13:3
He who guards his mouth preserves his life,
but he who opens wide his lips shall have destruction.

Are you guarding your mouth? Are you thinking about what is about to come out holding back words that never need to be heard? There is an old saying, "Bite Your Tongue." If that's what it takes it may not be a bad idea. Let's go one step further, from holding back, to replacing those words, with what God said.

The book of wisdom, Proverbs, speaks on this subject. Please turn there and discover what God says about our words. There are blanks for the results from bad or negative words and from good or positive words spoken. Please fill in each accordingly. (I started you off)

Proverbs 13:3
Good/Positive - <u>preserves own life</u>
Bad/Negative - <u>shall have destruction</u>

Proverbs 15:4
Good/Positive - _____
Bad/Negative - _____

Proverbs 16:23-24
Good/Positive - _____

There is one I want you to see in the New Testament spoken by Jesus.

Matthew 12:37
Good/Positive - _____
Bad/Negative - _____

I pray you have a vivid and fresh understanding of the power of the words that we speak. I also pray that you will realize this power affects every aspect of your life. Not only do we need to speak His word about our healing, but over our futures, our children, their futures, our spouses, you name it, if it's in your life you need to speak His word about it.

TODAY'S MEMORY VERSE:
PROVERBS 18:21
Death and life are in the power of the tongue, and those who love it will eat its fruit.

Be Blessed!

QUEST JOURNAL

Use this section as a reflection of your journey with God or write your prayer about where you've been and where you're going next.

_____

_____

_____

_____

_____

_____

_____

_____

_____

_____

_____

_____

_____

_____

_____

_____

_____

_____

_____

_____

_____

_____

_____

_____

_____

_____

_____

_____

_____

_____

Week 5

Saturate Everything in His Word Through the Three P's.

When talking about something that goes together, my Mother will say, "they fit together like three peas in a pod." That is exactly what we have here, Three P's in a pod. Praises, promises, and prayer all wrapped up in a pod of believing.

Day 1: Praises And Believe

PSALM 22:3
But you are holy, enthroned in the praises of Israel.

Praise
1) the act of expressing approval or admiration; commendation; laudation
2) the offering of grateful homage in words or song, as an act of worship.

Above is The Random House College Dictionary definition of praise. In the Psalm 22:3 Scripture passage, we learn God is enthroned in the praises of Israel. Israel is God's chosen people. If you have believed in Jesus as Lord and Savior, You are God's chosen as well. The original Hebrew word for enthroned, as used in Psalm 22:3, means to dwell, to remain, sit, or abide. God is dwelling, remaining, sitting, and abiding in the praises of His people, namely, you and me.

PSALM 33:12
Blessed is the nation whose God is the Lord,
the people He has chosen as His own inheritance.

Please write your name in the blank below.

God has chosen _____

Please do not take offense. I am in no way trying to insult your intelligence by making the same point over and over, but rather, I see it as crucial to drive the point deep in our minds that we are God's chosen people.

I love David. He made such a mess of his life, yet God still called him, *"a man after My own heart" (Acts 13:22)*. I believe Psalm 34:1-3 reveals at least one reason God would speak such precious words about His chosen, David.

Read Psalm 34:1-3.

Please fill in the words that David said about God.

I will bless the Lord _____ _____ _____ .

His praise shall _____ be in my mouth.

David knew God and knew He was praise worthy all the time, no matter what he was going through or experiencing. And David did face dire circumstances during his life. He lost his firstborn. Another son turned against him and tried to kill him. Another enemy, Saul, sought to kill him and David was forced to hide in caves. He also suffered from disease and other distresses. But David knew his circumstances, no matter how dire, did not change God. God is good. Let's look at what David had to say about all his distresses and God at the end of his life.

Read 1ˢᵗ Kings 1:29 and fill in the blank.

"As the Lord lives, who has redeemed my life from _____ distress."

At the end of his life after many struggles, David is still praising the Lord. He realizes and declares that God was the one who had saved him from every one of those distresses.

What three things we can learn from David today?
1) God is always praise worthy.

2) God is in our praises.
3) God is the One who delivers us from all of our distresses.

Make a list of your reasons to praise God. What has He delivered you from? How has He helped you in the distant or recent past?

_____

_____

_____

_____

_____

_____

_____

We all have reasons to praise God; sometimes we simply need to remember.

Our last exercise involves sticky notes, or tape and paper. Find one or the other and write your memory verse on at least three of them. Post them where you will see them throughout your day. (It won't hurt to leave them there.)

My three daughters and I are busy with different church and extra curricular activities. This keeps me behind the wheel so I like to post scriptures on my car's dash board. Your mirror in your bathroom might be a good place, and on the door that you use most in your home. If you work, take one and post it in your sight. Keep them there as a reminder to tell the Lord of His worth and His works. He loves to hear you say it.

Today's Memory Verse:
PSALMS 9:1
I will praise You, O Lord with my whole heart; I will tell of all Your marvelous works.

───────────── ⁕ 🐚 ⁕ ─────────────

DAY 2: PROMISES AND BELIEVE

MATT. 8:16-17
When evening had come,
they brought to Him many who were demon-possessed.
And He cast out the spirits with a word,
and healed all who were sick,
that it might be fulfilled which was spoken by Isaiah the prophet,
saying: "He Himself took our infirmities and bore our sicknesses."

Matthew 8:17 sounds like a promise to me, and strikes a chord of an old hymn:
"Standing, standing,
standing on the promises of God, my Savior,
standing, standing,
I'm standing on the promises of God." [3]

God gave us promises to us stand on. Plant your feet Sister, and don't budge!

2ND CORINTHIANS 1:20
"For all the promises of God in Him are Yes,
and in Him Amen,
to the glory of God through us."

Yes! Yes! Yes! The promises of God are fulfilled in His son Jesus. Remember, we are going through a process of healing, on a quest for wholeness.

Read Exodus 15:26

Complete the statement God made to His people.

"For I am the Lord _____ _____ _____ ."
Travel down the road about seven centuries to the day of the prophet, Isaiah.

Read Isaiah 53:5

How does Isaiah say we are healed?

_____

_____

The word *heals* in Exodus 15:26 and *healed* in Isaiah 53:5 are the same word in the original Hebrew language, *rapha*. The Complete Word Study Dictionary defines *"rapha"* as *"A verb meaning to heal, to make fresh. It describes the process of healing, being restored to health, made healthy."*

In the body of Christ, controversy surrounds the topic of healing and health. I will explain my understanding; however, I do not want you to take my word for it. Seek God and allow Him to teach you. Some believe Isaiah 53:5 relates strictly to the spiritual healing that seals our eternal destiny; others believe it is about physical healing. On this issue I straddle the fence. I have sought God with my whole heart and I believe both. Yes, it's spiritual, first and above all. But I also believe there is physical and emotional healing wrapped in this package deal.

The greatest healing that will ever take place in a life is the spiritual healing of salvation. As Christians, we grasp the step from the soil of earth to streets of gold; eternal salvation. But many times we miss the healing which leads to wholeness on this side of eternity. Let's look at this package in terms of something tangible.

Let's say someone gives you the car of your dreams. It's the color you want, leather interior, has a sunroof, and all the bells and whistles. But, when you go to put the key in the ignition, you notice, there's not a steering wheel. Your dream car is in your garage, but you can't go anywhere in it because you can't steer it.

How would you feel about the missing steering wheel?

_____

_____

I see healing much like the missing steering wheel; a vital part of the package. Without it we miss a portion of the great benefits of our salvation. Let's shift gears and look at how much our healing meant to Jesus.

Just before Jesus was crucified, Pilate ordered Him to be beaten with a bone and metal laced whip. Isaiah foretold details of the beating's outcome the Messiah would take for the healing of all who would believe.

ISAIAH 52:14
Just as many were astonished at you,
So His visage was marred more than any man,
And His form more than the sons of men;

The word *astonished* in the original Hebrew language means *to be desolate, be appalled, stun, stupefy, causing horror. Visage* speaks of the *outward appearance. Marred* in Hebrew means *disfigurement.*

Looking back at Isaiah 52:14 and the original meaning of the words astonished, visage, and marred, rewrite this scripture in your own words.

_____

_____

_____

_____

Jesus did not take this promise lightly. Keeping the promise meant so much to Him that He was willing to suffer horrific torture. I pray you understand the magnitude of what Jesus did for our healing and that you are inspired to stand on the promises of God.

Today's Memory Verse:
ROMANS 4:21
And being fully convinced that what He had promised He was able to perform.

Day 3: Prayer And Believe (part 1)

JAMES 5:14
Is any sick among you?
Let him call for the elders of the church;
and let them pray over him,
anointing him with oil in the name of the Lord.

Here I go singing again. (On paper is the safest place for my singing!)
"What a friend we have in Jesus,
All our sins and grief to bear,
What a privilege to carry
Everything to God in prayer." [4]

Why the elders? The elders represent spiritual leadership. Elders have walked with the Lord for a long time and have experience on their side. They would be sure of whom God is, least likely to doubt, and most likely to believe that He is able to do what He says He can do.

Think about the mental, emotional, and physical state of the sick person. If it is a deadly disease, their minds may be bombarded with so much they can't think clearly. Their thoughts may be on future suffering, how their family will be affected, or wondering, "why me," or what they will look like without hair. They could be in pain or ill from treatments or medication. How much can that alter our ability to think and reason? Who knows, our imagination can run wild. Until we walk a mile in their shoes, we can only imagine.

Read Hebrews 2:14-18

Who does Jesus give aid to? (vs. 16)

If you need a reminder about who is the seed of Abraham flip back to Day 1 in this week and read Galatians 3:29.

Who did He have to be made like? (vs.17)

_____

That He might be a _____ and _____ High Priest.

Verse 18 speaks of His suffering. The original Greek meaning of *suffering* is to be affected or have been affected, to feel, have a sensible experience, to undergo in a good sense or bad sense or of a sick person. Christ did walk a mile in our shoes. He understands. So at our weakest point He tells us get help from those who are strong. Let's look at an example in Scripture.

Read Acts 14:19-23

Paul is stoned and left for dead and disciples gather around him. Can you imagine the words spoken in that circle of believers? "Thank you Jesus for the life that is in Paul." "Hey Paul, get up man, you will *'not die, but live and declare the works of the Lord.'" (Psalm 118:17)* "No weapon formed against you shall prosper." (Isaiah 54:17)* "Come on Paul, we have got places to go, people to save. God has a plan and He's not done with you yet. Thank you, Jesus, that by Your stripes Paul was healed." *(Isaiah 53:5)* The words may have been different, but I can't help believing the words spoken were God's words and encouraging words.

If the disciples had not been there believing and encouraging Paul at such a weak moment, it would have been easy for him to lay there and die. These are Paul's words in *Philippians 1:23, "For I am hard-pressed between the two having a desire to depart and be with Christ, which is far better."* Oh Yes, I believe it would have been very easy for Paul to give up this life to enter the next. But instead, Paul lives and goes on to preach the gospel.

Besides preaching the gospel what does verse 22 tell us Paul and Barnabas were doing?

_____

_____

_____

_____

_____

Jesus loves us so much He gives us brothers and sisters to lift us up when we are too down and out to do it on our own. He is so good and His loving kindness endures forever!

Today's Memory Verse:
ROMANS 8:35
Who shall separate us from the love of Christ? Shall tribulation, or distress, or persecution, or famine, or nakedness, or peril or sword?

———————————— ⚜ ————————————

DAY 4: PRAYER AND BELIEVE (PART 2)

JAMES 5:14
Is any sick among you?
Let him call for the elders of the church;
and let them pray over him,
anointing him with oil in the name of the Lord.

Yesterday, we investigated why to call the elders. Let's talk about prayer. In Week 1, Day 3 we talked about the disciples asking Jesus to increase their faith, today we will talk about another request they made of Him.

LUKE 11:1
Now it came to pass,
as He was praying in a certain place,
when He ceased, that one of His disciples said to Him,
"Lord, teach us to pray,
as John also taught his disciples."

The disciples had the awesome privilege of being with Jesus when He prayed to His Daddy. When Jesus prayed was He laughing from the delight of spending time with His father? Was He crying for those He would soon die for? The disciples saw something that must have been special because seeing Jesus pray made them ask how. For many of you this next part could be very familiar to you. I pray if this passage is well-known to you, you will be open and seek a fresh new word from the Lord today. Please stop and pray the prayer below.

Bright and Morning Star,
Let Your Fresh Morning Light shine down on me as I study how You taught us to pray. Let me see what you want me to see and hear what you want me to hear, this day. In the blessed name of Jesus I pray. Amen.

This is what Jesus taught:

The Lord's Prayer Luke 11:2-4

Our Father in Heaven hallowed be your name.

This is lifting up the Father, extolling Him, exalting Him and praising who He is. This is not for Him. He knows who He is. This is to remind us and keep us focused on who He is and what He can do. Remember, God is enthroned in our praises *(Psalm 22:3)*.

Your kingdom come, Your will be done on earth as it is in heaven.

This is asking for His will not our own. We can do this with confidence and trust as we come to know Him and know what He thinks about us.

74

Read and write down Jeremiah 29:11

_____

_____

_____

_____

_____

_____

Remember, He came for us to have the abundant life. *(John 10:10)*

Give us this day our daily bread.

Daily is a key word here. He is telling us to come to Him daily for our need and necessities in life. If you are coming to Him daily asking for your daily requirements for life you will not go without, He will supply all that you need, and there is no reason to worry.

Read Luke 12:22-31

And forgive our debts as we forgive our debtors.

This can be the hardest part of all, but I want you to write the name of the person who you need to forgive in the blank below. If you are not sure whether there is someone you have not forgiven, ask God; He will show you. We do not have the ability to forgive on our own. It is by His grace we are forgiven, and by His grace we are forgiving.

Read Matt. 6:14-15 (As you see, this is very important!)

I am willing to forgive _____
that I may be forgiven.

And do not lead us into temptation, but deliver us from the evil one.

We could avoid many temptations if we ask Him to keep us from them. In the garden of Gethsemane, Jesus told Peter to pray lest He enter into temptation *(Matthew 26:41)*. Peter slept. Within the next hour Jesus was betrayed to those who would put Him to death. Peter was cutting off a man's ear and soon after that emphatically denying that He ever knew Jesus. Prayer might have been a little more valuable to Him than sleep. How many times do we say, "I try to pray and I just fall asleep?" Find a time to pray that you can stay awake.

For yours is the kingdom the power and glory forever. Amen.

The focus settles on the Lord. This implies, "It is all about You, Lord." There is so much freedom in knowing that it is not about who I am or what I can do, but about Jehovah God – the Great I AM! Hallelujah!

Today's memory verse will be different, you choose it and write the one that speaks to you after studying this lesson. Seek God for what He wants to speak to you today.

Today's Memory Verse:

_____

_____

_____

_____

———————————— ❖ ⊛ ❖ ————————————

DAY 5: PRAYER AND BELIEVE (PART 3)

JAMES 5:14
Is any sick among you?
Let him call for the elders of the church;
and let them pray over him,
anointing him with oil in the name of the Lord.

Anointing with oil symbolizes the way healing comes. Compare salvation and water baptism. Water baptism is a symbol of the cleansing that is actually taking place in the spirit. It is something we can see and can hold on to when the enemy comes to place doubt in our mind. How many times did I hear the words ring in my ears, "You are not really saved." But once I was baptized, it gave me confidence to say, "Oh yes, I am!" Now I am quick to tell the enemy who he is messing with, a child of the Most High God, the One who has crushed his head.

I believe anointing with oil is similar. We can hold on to this step of obedience when the enemy comes to spread his evil lies in our mind. When he tells us we are really not healed, we can tell him, "Oh yes, I am! I did exactly what my Father in heaven told me to and I believe what He says is true and you are a liar so go dig a hole somewhere and bury your crushed head in it!" Sorry, I got a little carried away, but I sure do feel better. Who better to take your frustrations out on than the one who came to steal, kill, and destroy your life? *(John 10:10)*

The last words in James 5:14, "in the name of the Lord" is the power. *"For whoever calls on the name of the Lord shall be saved."* *(Romans 10:13)* Guess what I did. I looked up the original meaning of the word *saved* and found it means *to save, keep safe and sound, to rescue from danger or destruction, from injury or peril, to save a suffering one from perishing or disease, to make well, heal, restore to health, to save in the technical biblical sense, to deliver from the penalties of the Messianic judgment, to save from the evils which obstruct the reception of the Messianic deliverance.* Can you say, "Wow!"? Okay, I will. " Wow!"

Read Proverbs 18:10 and fill in the blanks.

The name of the Lord is a _____.
The _____ run to it and are safe.

Read Romans 4:20-22 and fill in these blanks.

Was there a promise? _____

Did Abraham waver through unbelief? _____

What was he strengthened in? _____

What did he give God? _____

How convinced was he that God was able to perform what He had promised? _____

Because of all of this, what was accounted to him? _____
_____

We are going to end today with a hilarious story in scripture.

Read Acts 19:11-17

Funny it may be, but there is a profound truth in the midst of this story. The truth is: Relationship truly does make the difference. These men did not know

Jesus, but they thought that they would try out the name in which they had seen many miracles performed. This turned out to be very dangerous for them. On the other hand if these men had of known Jesus, the evil spirits in that man would have tucked their tail and ran like a scalded dog. I thought you might have been up for another one of Mama's sayings.

Today's Memory Verse:
ACTS 4:30
"by stretching out your hand to heal, and that signs and wonders may be done through the name of Your holy servant Jesus."

Be Blessed!

QUEST JOURNAL

Use this section as a reflection of your journey with God or write your prayer about where you've been and where you're going next.

Week 6
All Terrain Vehicle

Everybody needs an ATV when going on a quest. The titles of the next 3 days begin with ATV. How fitting. The next five days we will learn about our All Terrain Vehicle that should go wherever we go, when we go, and as we go. This is a ride you won't want to miss.

DAY 1: ALWAYS WITHOUT CEASING

1 THESSALONIANS 5:16-18
Rejoice always, pray without ceasing,
in everything give thanks;
for this is the will of God in Christ Jesus for you.

Read Luke 10:17-20

What does Jesus give us authority over?

_____

What does Jesus say not to rejoice in?

_____

What does He say to rejoice in?

_____

List the reasons you think Jesus gave these instructions about what we should and should not rejoice in?

_____

_____

Jesus knows we would have the tendency to focus on the power. There is a fine line between operating in our power potential and allowing pride to draw us into thinking more about what "I" can do and what power "I" have. We might end up sounding more like the enemy than His child. Using His gift of authority is a must. Confidence in who we are is a must. But humility in how we are who we are is where our joy and rejoicing should be. We have reason to rejoice no matter what we face; He has done great things for us. So rejoice and move into prayer without ceasing.

Read Luke 11:5-8 and Luke 18:1-8.

In these stories what caused each to receive what they asked for?

_____

_____

Yes, you got it! Never give up! This reminds me of the first few months of my little girls' lives, how I would repeatedly say, "Say Mama." I could not wait for them to say it. And when they finally did, that was one of the most exciting times of my life. Now they say it so much that sometimes it wears me out. That's when they know they have got me and they make their move. When I have heard the word "Mama" a thousand times in the past 45 seconds (small exaggeration) is when I am most prone to say, "Okay! Okay! Whatever you want, just please don't say that name again." Thank God, He is much more tolerant and patient than we are. But persistence does pay off. My three girls will experience positively answered prayer, because they have this concept down to a fine art.

Has anyone ever asked you for something and they were so persistent that you gave them what they wanted?

_____

_____

Have you ever been persistent praying about something and God has given you what you asked for? If so, explain.

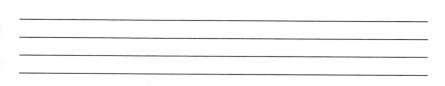

As you learn today's memory verse change Hannah's name to your own.

Today's Memory Verse:
1 SAMUEL 2:1
And <u>Hannah</u> prayed and said: My heart rejoices in the Lord; my horn is exalted in the Lord. I smile at my enemies, because I rejoice in Your salvation.

DAY 2: THANKFULNESS IN EVERYTHING

1 THESSALONIANS 5:16-18
Rejoice always, pray without ceasing,
in everything give thanks;
for this is the will of God in Christ Jesus for you.

I wonder if everything means everything.

EPHESIANS 5:20
Giving thanks always for all things unto God
and the Father in the name of our Lord Jesus Christ.

Everything, all things, sounds like the same thing.

Read 2 Corinthians 9:8-15.
Please list the three alls found in verse 8.

All _____

All _____

All _____

Verse 11 says we are enriched in everything to all liberality which causes _____ .

The Complete Word Study Dictionary defines *liberality* as used in verse 11 as *"faithful benevolence out of proper motivation."* Random House College Dictionary defines benevolence as the desire to do good to others; good will or charitableness.

We are enriched in everything to all faithful desire to do good to others out of a right motivation which causes thanksgiving.

Rewrite verse 11 in your own words.

_____

_____

God has given us all that we need for every circumstance. He has made a way, whether on the mountaintop or in the lowest valley, whether feast or famine. He gives us grace sufficient for all things that we may face and His indescribable gift of grace causes us to be thankful. Paul, the author of all the Scriptures we have read today believed we should be thankful in everything, good or bad.

Read 2 Corinthians 12:7-10

Did God remove Paul's throne in the flesh?

_____

What did God say to Paul? (vs.9)

_____

_____

The next verse Paul is saying that he is glad even takes pleasure in his infirmity, in reproaches, in necessity, in persecutions, in distresses for Christ sake. Paul truly understood the meaning of giving thanks in everything.

PSALM 100:4
Enter into His gates with thanksgiving,
and into His courts with praise.
Be thankful to Him and bless His name.

Why does giving thanks matter? If you are thankful it changes who you are and the choices you make. Being thankful for what Jesus has done and is doing in my life has changed who I am and the choices I make. One leper's thankfulness among ten healed lepers caused him to make different choices. *(Luke 17:15-16)* Thankfulness is uncontainable and moves us to action. It moved the leper to return, give God glory, and fall on His face in worship. Thankfulness is what moves me to live my life fully for Him and to do that with joy and gladness. It causes me to dance in my home, and sing in my car.

Jesus dying for me is above all the first thing I am most thankful for. I believe thankfulness is a gift in itself because thankfulness only came once I ever realized who Jesus is and what He did for me. Thankfulness is a direct result of what I call, "The Hot Pursuit of Jesus." Looking back on a life filled with sin, I see a life Jesus never gave up on. I see Jesus in hot pursuit of me even in the darkest hours. I realize He was pursuing me when many would have said, "Hopeless", but He said, "Precious". He saw my life as valuable and precious, not because of me, but I was His *"fearfully and wonderfully made"* creation *(Psalm 139:14)..* Whether we acknowledge Him or not, does not change the fact that everything is ultimately about Jesus. How freeing is this simple fact!

Jesus is the most valuable precious gift of all! The knowledge that He, God and Man, during my darkest hour, hung mutilated, shamed, and forsaken by His Father, on a blood soaked cross for my sake changes everything. How can I, but love Him? I do love Him. He is all I need. He is the air I breathe, and He is life.

Are you so thankful for something that it changes who you are and the choices you make? Briefly explain.

_____

_____

_____

_____

What action has that thankfulness motivated you to take?

_____

_____

_____

When in your life do you recognize the overflow from the thankfulness?

_____

_____

_____

_____

Today's Memory Verse:
1 CORINTHIANS 15:57
But thanks be to God, who gives us the victory through our Lord Jesus Christ.

--------------- ❊ ⚙ ❊ ---------------

DAY 3: VOW OF FAITH

JAMES 5:15
And the prayer of faith will save the sick,
and the Lord will raise him up.
And if he has committed sins,
he will be forgiven.

Faith, faith and more faith! Faith is everywhere I turn as I am studying on the subject of healing and wholeness. The original

Greek meaning of the word, *prayer*, as used in James 5:15 is *a prayer to God or a vow*. This is the only time in Scripture this word is used for the word prayer with this meaning. This leads me to believe there is something exceptional about this prayer.

A vow is a pledge or commitment to something. In this case the something is faith. The prayer of faith is a pledge or commitment to faith. When You pray this prayer you are saying, "No matter what I think, hear, see or feel, I will put my trust in God." In the belly of a big fish, Jonah makes his own vow to the Lord.

Read Jonah 2:1-10

In the nine verses of this prayer Jonah made declarations in his hopeless state. He realized God was his only salvation. Jonah cries out to the Lord and reviews his circumstances. Then he makes his vow in verse 4. My translation: "I don't see any way that you can see me, but I am going to keep looking to You." His next vow is in verse 6.

What is your translation of Jonah's vow in verse 6?

_____

_____

_____

_____

Jonah was in a situation that any could say was doomed to failure, but he vowed that his trust was in the Lord. The last vow of the prayer, Jonah says, "...I will pay what I have vowed..."(vs. 9). The word *pay*, means *to be in a covenant of peace.*

What is the final sentence in Jonah's prayer? (vs.9)

_____

_____

What do you think Jonah meant when he said he would pay what he vowed?

_____

_____

_____

_____

Chances any of us will ever be in the belly of a fish are slim to none. But it's probable that we will face a situation in which there is no way out, or at the very least, desperate. Will we make a vow that we will be at peace with God and trust Him. Or will we curl under a tree somewhere as Elijah did in 1 Kings 19:4 and say, Just go ahead and kill me, Lord I can't take it any longer.

Please know that I am not knocking Elijah. I love Elijah. He gives me so much hope, because I can so relate to him. One minute I am full of faith ready to conquer all that I may face in the name of Jesus and with His sword. Then before I know it I am groveling before the Lord, declaring that I am too big of a mess that He should give up on me. "Oh me of little faith. That's it. I said it!" When we turn things around to be about "me" is when we lose heart.

Write your own vow of faith to the Lord. It may be a vow you need right now or for what you will face tomorrow. But now is the time to establish your vow of faith, that when desperate times come, you do as Jonah did in verse 7 and remember the Lord. My Vow of Faith:

_____

_____

_____

_____

_____

_____

_____

_____

_____

_____

_____

Today's Memory Verse:
PSALM 18:2
The Lord is my rock and my fortress and my deliverer; my God, my strength, in whom I will trust; my shield and the horn of my salvation, my stronghold.

———————————— ⁂ ————————————

DAY 4: SINS FORGIVEN

JAMES 5:15
And the prayer of faith will save the sick,
and the Lord will raise him up.
And if he has committed sins,
he will be forgiven.

Today, let's start reading Mark 2:1-12.

What caused Jesus to speak to the paralytic?

_____

_____

What word's did Jesus speak?

_____

_____

Scripture does not tell us any words spoken by this paralytic to declare his vow to God, but Jesus knew his commitment to believing in Him. If he could speak I am quite sure he told those who carried him, a list of, "no matter whats." "No matter what, you can not stop until we see Jesus." "No matter what, you can't bring me back home on this bed." "We are going through the roof if we have to, but I am going to see Jesus no matter what." Jesus saw the faith of those who brought the paralytic to Him. I think each of them declared a list of committed "no matter whats." If Jesus could see their faith, can He see ours? Do other people see our faith? Real faith is visible.

Is there a specific time in your life that you know your faith was so evident that it was visible? If so, explain.

_____

_____

_____

_____

What was the first words Jesus said to the paralytic?

_____

_____

Viewing our sins as forgiven is necessary to walk in wholeness. There is a correlation to us spiritually. If we don't recognize and accept that our sins are forgiven, those sins will keep us paralyzed. This is from the voice of experience. I have so much experience in this area I would go so far to say that I am an expert on this subject.

The first four years of my journey with the Lord I could do little more than show up to church on Sunday and hope that God would at least give me a janitor's position in heaven. The sin I had been forgiven of, yet still carried with me everywhere, was paralyzing me from truly loving and serving Him. It hindered my faith in every area.

It was not until I understood the gift of grace and that His blood covered all my sin that I was able to let go of the sin and fully grab hold of Jesus allowing Him to remove my chains until I was able to walk in wholeness, lift my hands in worship, dance with joy, and serve without shame.

Is there sin from the distant or not so distant past that you need to let go of because it is paralyzing you?

_____

Now is the time for freedom. Give it over into the hands of Jesus.

Write a prayer asking God to help you with letting go of the past and your commitment to believing Jesus' blood covers all your sin that you may walk in the freedom He died for you to have.

_____

_____

_____

_____

_____

_____

_____

My dear sister and friend, you are free in Jesus name! Walk like it, talk like it, and live like it!

Today's Memory Verse:
ROMANS 8:2
For the law of the Spirit of life in Christ Jesus has made me free from the law of sin and death.

———————— ❖ ⑮ ❖ ————————

DAY 5: CONFESSION

JAMES 5:16
Confess your trespasses to one another,
and pray for one another,
that you may be healed.
The effective, fervent prayer of a righteous man avails much.

This is one of those lessons that you may wish we could remove, but if we do, we might be way too comfortable in all of our faith talk. If you think about it and are honest about it, talking about faith is a little easier than confessing our sins to others. God thought it was important and did not remove it. So let's dig in.

A few years ago, I had a situation in church in which I fervently disagreed with a brother in Christ. In the beginning he asked my opinion and I gave it to him, but that did not change the situation. This was strictly an issue on how something should be done in the context of church. I did not say anything else because I thought it would only create strife and division so I left it alone. But I got more angry as time went on, to the point that I was hardly able to look at the man.

One day he had enough working together under such conditions, and he did the one thing that was more than I could take. He sent me a card saying he recognized I was hurt and apologized that he had any part of hurting me. He was also confrontational in a very loving manner. He reminded me of the fact that there were others much more vulnerable than us watching and that how we acted could cause someone else to stumble.

The Holy Spirit broke my heart that day. If you have ever had a holy spanking this was one of those. I picked up the phone and called my brother in Christ to confess to him how horrible I had acted. I cried and begged for his forgiveness and that changed everything, or almost. I say almost, because the way things were being done at church did not change much, but everything else did. I don't have a single negative feeling about the man, instead I love him. Jesus poured out grace on that situation that changed my perspective about a man that is God's child just like me. What I hope you get out of my confession is that confession changes who we are. Confession brings freedom, compassion, love and understanding.

Bible time! Read Colossians 3:12-16

What does God expect our behavior to be? (vs. 12-13)

_____

_____

_____

What does verse 15 say we were called to?

_____

_____

We are called to be one body. When that body has a problem like the one my brother and I had, it was like getting a wound and covering it with a band-aid, thinking, out of sight, out of mind. Absolutely not the case, because the wound was never cleansed or cared for, so it only festered and grew. This little bitty wound could have grown into something much worse if someone had not taken the time to recognize it and treat it. I am thankful that he was willing to recognize it and treat it when I was too wrapped up in me to do it myself.

Please read Hebrews 12:14-15.

Do you have a confession that you need to make?

_____

_____

To whom do you need to make the confession?

_____

_____

Are you willing to take a step of faith and make the confession?

_____

If you make this confession, record your feelings and changes because of it.

_____

_____

_____

_____

Today's Memory Verse:
JOHN 13:35
By this all will know that you are my disciples that you have love for one another.

Be Blessed!

QUEST JOURNAL

Use this section as a reflection of your journey with God or write your prayer about where you've been and where you're going next.

_____
_____
_____
_____
_____
_____
_____
_____
_____
_____
_____
_____
_____
_____
_____
_____
_____
_____
_____
_____
_____
_____
_____
_____
_____
_____

Week 7
Five Days of Healing

Congratulations! You have made it to the final week of study. I am so proud of you. This week we will look at different types of healings from Scripture. Healing is not only physical, though it is. It's not only emotional, though it is that as well. You may need healing in your home, your family, your marriage, your finances, etc. God's healing touch makes whole whatever is broken.

Day 1: Household Healed

PROVERBS 19:23
The fear of the Lord leads to life,
and he who has it will abide in satisfaction;
he will not be visited with evil.

Please read Genesis 20:1-18

What description did God use about Abimelech's heart? (vs.6)

_____

_____

God knew the motive of Abimelech's heart and kept him from sinning against Him. This is a prime example of the justness and trustworthiness of God. Once Abimelech knew the truth, he had a choice; obedience or disobedience, blessing or curse.

What reason did Abraham give Abimelech about why he had withheld the truth from him?

_____

_____

How did Abimelech and his servants feel in verse 8?

_____

_____

PROVERBS 9:10
*"The fear of the Lord is the beginning of wisdom,
and the knowledge of the Holy One is understanding."*

Fear of the Lord may have been missing when Abraham stepped foot on Abimelech's property, but fear of the Lord came when God spoke. It's so cool to me that God used Abraham's mess up to reveal Himself to others who did not know Him. Abimelech feared God and chose obedience and blessing. His wife and female servants were healed. Their wombs were opened.

On Week 3, Day 1, 2, and 3, we studied three reasons why God gives us the things we ask. (It's okay to peek.) They were:
1) Commandments _____
2) God _____
3) That our _____ may be full

The commandment was kept. God was glorified. Did God's blessing cause their joy to be full?

PROVERBS 3:13
*"Happy is the man who finds wisdom,
and the man who gains understanding."*

Read Psalm 113:9 / Who is described as joyful?

_____

_____

Read Psalm 127:3-5

What understanding do you gain about children?

_____

_____

What do these Psalms lead you to believe about Abimelech's and His family's joy?

_____

_____

Picture Abimelech's household healed.

Can you see the children running through the house with squeals of laughter? Little girls sing to baby dolls and feed them mud pies Mischievous boys hide watching, sticks poised as bow and arrow, waiting for the next unsuspecting victim; Dad. He enters the room and whistles pierce the quiet. The young son jumps on Dad's back as he innocently strolls through the room. The war is on! Son number two captures Dad around his ankles. The oldest rounds the corner. Dad grabs him as he falls to the floor. War hoops sound out as all are alerted to the fact that the wrestling match of the day has now begun and one by one they heave themselves atop the family heap. Mom chuckles. Her home is as it should be full of life and joy.

Today's Memory Verse: *Psalm 147:11*
The Lord takes pleasure in those who fear Him, in those who hope in His mercy.

DAY 2: BITTER MADE SWEET

PSALM 63:1
O God, You are my God;
Early will I seek You;

My flesh longs for You in a dry and thirsty land
where there is no water.

This lesson may be as hard for some of us to swallow as the water of Marah was for the Israelites. But here we go, choking or not. The story is of a healing, but of a different nature than a physical healing. The story begins right after God has delivered the Israelites from the hand of Pharaoh, through the middle of the Red Sea on dry ground. God then drowns their enemies in the Red Sea while they were in pursuit of His chosen.

Read Exodus 15:22-26

Verse 23 says, "for they were bitter." Who or what was bitter?

_____

_____

I always thought it was the water that was bitter, but today I had to wonder if it was the people, not the water, or both. When I was a junior in high school (That was a long time ago!) my English teach had a sign posted on her door saying: "Attitudes are contagious." I've also heard people say, "That attitude might rub off onto someone else." How about this old saying, "You need a taste of your own medicine." It seems they may have gotten just that. I'll try to go easy on the Israelites, so we might have to take a bit of the brunt for them.

"For Instance"

You had a great day yesterday, everything that could have or might have gone wrong turned out for your good. You went to bed dancing and singing, but it's Monday morning. You sleep through the alarm, skip breakfast and run out the door. Your first appointment of the day and you're late. Those waiting for you aren't doing so patiently. You try to put on your best smile hoping you can fake it until you feel it. The day is a whirl wind. Nothing is easy. The phone rings, and rings, and rings. Your well meaning friend stops by to "chat." It's two o'clock in the afternoon your stomach is roaring, and your head feels like it might split down the middle. If that's not enough, your boss is breathing down your neck about an impossible deadline. "With God all things are possible," has drowned in the midst of a day's happenings. By the time you get back home it is 7pm and not a bite all day. What is your disposition?

Let's take another for instance. Just say, for one reason or another you don't get to eat that night and the next two days repeat the one before. Do you think that your attitude and outlook may have turned a slight bit bitter?

In all fairness, the Israelites had less to keep them occupied from thinking about their dry parched mouth than we would in our busy lives today. The sad thing in both instances is the need for God, but too preoccupied with what we experience and feel to stop and say, *As the deer pants for the water brooks, so pants my soul for You, O God."(Psalm 42:1)* Didn't they know the God who had parted the Red Sea for them to cross on dry ground only days before could have provided them water? I guess not. They looked to Moses. Moses cried out to God.

The waters were made sweet. God commanded the Israelites to keep His commandments, and He would keep them disease free. And I do believe they were full of joy when they put the sweet water to their dry cracked lips.

Can you think of a time when you were bitter and now realize if you had cried out to God instead of complaining about your circumstances you could have seen God intervene and replace that bitterness with sweet water? Explain.

_____

_____

_____

_____

Ask God to use this as a teaching tool and remind you of it whenever you are tempted to get bitter about circumstances beyond your control, but not His.

Today's Memory Verse:
ISAIAH 59:1
Behold the Lord's hand is not shortened that it cannot save; nor His ear heavy that it cannot hear.

———————— ❧ ❀ ❧ ————————

DAY 3: MADE WHOLE

JAMES 1:4
*But let patience have its perfect work,
that you may be perfect and complete, lacking nothing.*

We are almost finished and I have felt hard-pressed to show the perfect healing story for today. Not that any healing is not perfect, because we know that all healing comes from God, and He is perfect. In elementary Math class fact families are taught.

You can call this a holy fact family:
Healing = God's Work
God's Work = Perfection
Perfection = Healing
God's Work = Perfection = Healing

Elementary Math Fact Family
2+3=5   5-3=2
3+2=5   5-2=3

Mark 5:25-34 has this equation woven into the fabric of every hem. Please read it very carefully making sure not to skim over any precious details.

How long had her affliction lasted? _____
How much had it cost her? _____

What was her condition after all the expense and suffering?

_____

Jesus was in town. It was now or never, she had to make a choice and she had to have a "no matter what" kind of attitude. She sets her face like flint and shoves her way through the crowd, an unclean woman, destitute, and helpless, yet not hopeless. It must have began as just a glimmer, but hope increases as she stirs herself up and sets her faith goal, *"If only I may touch His clothes, I shall be made well."*

Her faith had a goal. His clothes were the goal or the point at which she had set in her heart that she could be healed. For each of us our faith goal is different. Just think about the Roman Centurion that caused Jesus to marvel. Never mind, don't just think about it.

Read Luke 7:1-10.

What was the Centurion's faith goal? _____

_____

Do you have a faith goal set for a touch or a miracle you are seeking God for in your life? If so what?

_____

_____

_____

_____

It is marvelous to see where the centurion had set his faith goal, on the spoken word of God. His faith surely was to be marveled at, if even Jesus would marvel. But there is something special in the faith goal of the woman. The woman had been unclean for twelve years, in Jewish law, that meant untouchable. No wonder her faith goal involved the touch. How she must have longed for the touch. How long since she had felt anything other than suffering?

But this was a new day. She is healed by faith in a Man whom she dared to touch. And how sweet He is – He let's her feel her healing. I have heard, "We walk by faith not by feeling." Please don't misunderstand me, I do believe we walk by faith. But I also believe there are times we come so close to Christ His presence is felt. These intimate moments can come whether at home bowed before Him, or in corporate worship at church, or even, driving down the road singing His praises. Sometimes we feel His presence as we seek Him through Bible study. I love that feeling and there is healing in His presence.

Think back to the equation. Of course this was a healing, and this healing was obviously God's Work. What about perfection? The scripture says that she was made whole. Made whole means nothing missing, nothing broken. Her healing was perfect. He told her to go in peace. Why? Because - He had healed her completely.

What else could His healing have touched in her life besides the issue of blood?

_____

_____

_____

_____

What else could His healing touch in your life besides the main most evident issue?

_____

_____

_____

_____

Today's Memory Verse:
3 JOHN 2
Beloved, I pray that you may prosper in all things and be in health, just as your soul prospers.

_____ ❖ ⟨☙⟩ ❖ _____

DAY 4: WITH ONE ACCORD

ACTS 5:31
And when they had prayed,
the place where they were assembled was shaken;
and they were all filled with the Holy Spirit,
and they spoke the word of God with boldness.

There is so much to say, and this will only be a glimpse. Today we are going to look at how ordinary people used by God to perform God-sized miracles. They were God-sized because they were all God. These ordinary people were working under the power of the Holy Spirit. The same Spirit in Jesus, the same Spirit who moved upon the face of the waters at creation, and the same Spirit who empowered weak men all through out the Bible to accomplish impossible tasks.

ACTS 5:15
So that they brought the sick out into the streets
and laid them on beds and couches,
that at least the shadow of Peter passing by might fall on them.

Wow! That is so powerful! The original Greek meaning for the word *shadow* is totally cool. *Shadow* means *shade caused by the interception of light; an image cast by an object and representing the form of that object.*

Do you think Peter was intercepting the light of Christ?

Was the image of Christ so cast on Peter that he was representing the fullness of Jesus? What are your thoughts?

_____

_____

_____

_____

_____

In Acts 3 Peter empowered by the Holy Spirit and in the name of Jesus heals a forty year old man, lame since birth. The apostles healed many as recorded in Acts. I want to understand what the apostles knew and were doing that we obviously are missing out on. I may step on a few toes today, but just know I can't even walk for stepping on my own in this.

Read these different passages, what is the same in each of them?

Acts 2:1
They were all _____ in one place.

Acts 2:46
So continuing daily _____ in the temple

Acts 4:24
They raised their voice to God _____ and said: "Lord, You are God, who made heaven and earth and the sea, and all that is in them.

Acts 5:12
And through the hands of the apostles many signs and wonders were done among the people. And they were all _____ in Solomon's Porch.

Do you get the idea? They were focused on one thing - Jesus. They were loving, serving, and obeying Him. Different personalities, preferences, opinions did not matter or rule, only Jesus. They were focused and purpose driven people. The last thing they were thinking of was getting there on time to sit in the seat they had claimed as their own. If that not you, let's try this one. "If they don't play the music I like, I'm going somewhere that does." Okay! Okay! Just one more. "Well, Suzie Q really hurt my feelings today and I just don't know if I can keep going there."

Are your extremely uncomfortable now? As my mama would say, "Don't get all bent out of shape." I can relate these things to you because I have had to face and deal with them. I'm not pointing fingers. My question is, "Where are the Holy Spirit's fingers pointing?" Any of this strike you as convicting? You may have a different hindrance to being with one accord with your brothers and sisters in Christ.

What is your greatest hindrance(s) to being with one accord in the body of Christ?

_____

_____

_____

This is not easy, but it's important. I have always told my daughters the people with the most problems are those who think they don't have problems. Until we admit where we struggle we can't be made whole. Facing and dealing with our issues is the first step toward wholeness. I hope you have been able to do come clean with the Lord during this study. If so, you are well on your way in your quest for wholeness.

Commit to the Lord your willingness to have your heart changed forever.

_____

_____

_____

Why all the fuss about "with one accord"? We are one body, if we want to operate in power, we must do it the way the body was designed to function, all together with one focus and one purpose.

Read and meditate on Acts 4:32-35. What is God speaking to you?

_____

_____

_____

_____

Today's Memory Verse:

ROMANS 15:5&6
Now may the God of patience and comfort grant you to be like-minded toward one another, according to Christ Jesus, that you may with one mind and one mouth glorify God and Father of our Lord Jesus Christ.

DAY 5: ULTIMATE HEALING

REV. 22:4
"And God will wipe away every tear from their eyes;
there shall be no more death,
nor sorrow, nor crying.
There shall be no more pain,
for the former things have passed away."

God's plan has never been brokenness and pain but because of sin we fell out of God's perfect will for our lives. Sin is a result of our fallen nature yet all our offenses toward God are covered and removed by the powerful work of the cross. Jesus did all that He did, to get us back to the perfect way God planned for us, before creation. However, there are times God uses suffering and disease for His purposes.

Have you ever seen anyone suffer brokenness or sickness and could see God at work in the midst of the pain? Give an example.

_____

_____

_____

_____

ROMANS 8:28
And we know that all things work together
for good to those who love God,
To those who are called according to His purpose.

Yes, we may experience broken hearts, broken bodies, or broken lives, but we must stop accepting it and search for what God is doing in our lives and the live of those we know and love. Believe Him for all that He has promised us, and know that as we trust Him and love Him, He is working the circumstances of our lives out for our good.

Have you ever experienced pain that you can look back on and see that God worked it out for your good?

_____

_____

Have you experience God's healing touch in your life?

_____

_____

How I long for the day of the ultimate healing. The ultimate healing takes us back to the way God created everything to be in the beginning. The tree of life was seen in the midst of the Garden of Eden in Genesis 2:9, and there was no curse. This final healing is for all who came to Him on the earth side of eternity, found in Revelation 22, the last chapter in the Bible. Jesus is the Beginning and the End. He is our Healer and He is perfection.

Refresh your memory of the way it all began for man in the Garden of Eden.

Read Genesis 2:8-10 and 3:8 and Revelation 22:1-5

Now compare these two pictures. What is the same?

_____

_____

_____

_____

What will it be like in eternity? Living water, tree of life, and God Himself right smack dab in the middle of it all. What won't it be like in eternity? No curse, no sun, no sadness or sickness, and no sin or separation. In the past five days there have been two men that I have known most of my life who were very sick with disease and have now gone home to be with the Lord. They each suffered greatly their last days here on earth, but all that is gone now. They are in the presence of God Almighty. Even in their death, death had no victory over them, because they each knew Jesus as Lord and Savior. Death for them was the entrance to a spectacular and glorious eternity of perfection and wholeness like nothing we have ever imagined, even in our wildest dreams.

Read 1 Corinthians 15:54-58

Write verse 58 for your own encouragement.

_____

_____

_____

My prayer is that these words of Paul would be forever inscribed on your heart and mind, and will be a spur against complacency knowing your labor is not in vain.

ZEPHANIAH 1:12
And it shall pass at that time that I will punish the men
who are settled in complacency who say in their heart,
"The Lord will not do good, nor will He do evil."

This warning in Zephaniah reminds me of a similar one in Revelation.

Read Revelation 3:14-22

What one word did Jesus use to describe the Laodecian church? _____

Being aware of potential trouble helps us know what way to go or not to go. Hosea 4:6 states that God's *"people perish for lack of knowledge."* We now have a greater knowledge of God's word. His word leads to wholeness. However, your quest is not over because you're still breathing. So my dear Sister in Christ, stir yourself up, trust Him, believe Him, and live life extreme for Jesus. I want you to need a warning label, "Caution Contents Hot."

I am so proud of you for sticking it out to the end. I know you are well on our way to wholeness as you have sought God for that work in your life these past seven weeks. May God bless you, change you, and fill you to overflowing. Now that you have received, it is your turn to share what God has given to you. I love you and many prayers have been lifted to heaven for those who are reading these words.

Today's Memory Verse:
1 Corinthians 2:9

But it is written: "Eye has not seen, nor ear heard, nor have entered into the heart of man the things which God has prepared for those who love Him.

Be Blessed!

QUEST JOURNAL

Use this section as a reflection of your journey with God or write your prayer about where you've been and where you're going next.

_____

_____

_____

_____

_____

_____

_____

_____

_____

_____

_____

_____

_____

_____

_____

_____

_____

_____

_____

_____

_____

_____

_____

_____

_____

_____

_____

_____

_____

_____

_____

_____

ENDNOTES

[1] *Oh, How He Loves You and Me*
Words and Music: Kurt Kaiser
Copyright 1975 by Word Music a division of Word Inc.
Permission requested.

[2] *Down in My Heart*
Words and Music: George W. Cook
Public Domain

[3] *Standing on the Promises*
Words and Music: Kelso Carter - 1886
Public Domain

[4] *What A Friend We Have In Jesus*
Words: Joseph M. Scriven – 1855
Music: Charles C. Converse - 1868
Public Domain